THE TRIUMPH OF FAITH IN HABAKKUK

The Triumph of Faith in HABAKKUK

Donald E. Gowan

JOHN KNOX PRESS
ATLANTA

Scripture quotations in this publication are from the following:
From the *Revised Standard Version Bible,* copyright 1946, 1952, and © 1971 by the Division of Christian Education, National Council of the Churches of Christ in the U.S.A. and used by permission.

From *The New English Bible.* © The Delegates of the Oxford University Press and the Syndics of The Cambridge University Press, 1961, 1970.

From the Today's English Version of the New Testament. Copyright © American Bible Society 1966.

Acknowledgment is also made to quote from the following:
"God's Redeeming Love," by I.T. Bradley, in *Perspective* 13 (1972), 118–126. Published by Pittsburgh Theological Seminary.

Man Is Not Alone, by Abraham Heschel. Copyright © 1951 Farrar, Straus & Young; used by permission of Farrar, Straus & Giroux, Inc.

The Modern Message of the Minor Prophets, by Raymond Calkins. Copyright © 1947 Harper; used by permission of Harper & Row, Inc.

The Mountain That Moved, by Edward England. Copyright © 1967 Wm. B. Eerdmans Publishing Co. Used by permission.

Library of Congress Cataloging in Publication Data

Gowan, Donald E
   The triumph of faith in Habakkuk.

   Bibliography: p.
   1. Bible. O.T. Habakkuk—Criticism, interpretation, etc. I. Title.
BS1635.2.G68   224'.95'066   75–32843
ISBN 0–8042–0195–1

Dedicated to the memory of my father and mother

ELMER AND LUCILE GOWAN

whose lives revealed to many

what is meant by

"the just shall live by his faith"

Preface

Books on the problem of suffering continue to be written, for every generation encounters pain for itself and struggles to find the reason why. This little book makes no pretense of being a definitive treatment of the age-old questions, but has been produced in the conviction that the book of Habakkuk contains a message about how to live triumphantly in the midst of trouble which may be of help to some. Habakkuk tends to be overlooked in discussions of the question of theodicy and the problem of suffering—I believe because of its brevity rather than because what it says is unimportant. It is not that Old Testament scholars have neglected the book for there is an abundant literature on it, but there have remained two lacunae in recent publications. First, the newer developments in scholarship which have appeared in technical literature are not yet readily accessible to those outside the academic world (partly because so few commentaries in English on the minor prophets have appeared in recent years). And second, the commentaries and other studies of Habakkuk which do exist concentrate on the historical, philological and literary-critical problems it presents (and they are many) without treating its theology at any length. This book is a modest effort to contribute something in these two areas. It does not attempt to present a survey of recent research but will use the advances which have been made as aids to an improved understanding of Habakkuk's message. It frankly leaves to one side many of the difficult critical questions which the book presents—they are discussed at length in the commentaries—but does so not as a claim that they are unimportant but in the belief that they need not all be solved before we can say anything about what the book means. Scholars will recognize where I have followed one line of research and rejected another and will know to whom I am indebted for the positions taken on critical questions. Since the book is not addressed primarily to scholars, however, and since most of the relevant literature is in languages other than English, I have not provided the documentation which would be expected in a technical monograph. The translations of the Hebrew text of Habakkuk which I have provided are intended as an aid to the general reader, to be used alongside the standard translations, and are presented without text-critical or philological notes, although the rationale for the decisions made in producing them could be provided in another place.

I must express my appreciation here to two gentlemen mentioned in the book for the parts they played in its origin, Professor Joseph L. Mihelic and Dr. William Jackson, and to others over the years, who cannot be named here, whose personal "discoveries" of Habakkuk persuaded me that my feelings about the value of the book were not an unreasonable idiosyncrasy. Finally, my thanks go to Mrs. Jean Hadidian for her gracious assistance in typing the manuscript for me.

Pittsburgh Theological Seminary   Donald E. Gowan
September, 1975

Contents

CHAPTER I

WHY HABAKKUK?

Why should Habakkuk, that small and obscure part of the Old Testament tucked away somewhere in the middle of the minor prophets, deserve a book expounding its message? Is it perhaps because the exposition of favorites such as Isaiah, Genesis, and the Psalms has exhausted itself so that there is nothing new to say about those beloved books? Hardly. Seldom in history have so many new insights into the meaning of the best known parts of the Old Testament been forthcoming as in this latter half of the twentieth century. Could it then be a manifestation of a type of infracaninaphilia (a word somebody made up, meaning love of the underdog); trying to gain fame for a minor leaguer who may very well deserve to remain in the minors? I think I can defend myself against that charge. It is clear that Habakkuk, because of its brevity and the history of its use, has no ground for claiming that it ought to be a more central document in the Bible than it has been.

Yet there are reasons for offering a new interpretation of Habakkuk, and I believe they are sound. They are personal—growing out of the effect which the book has had on me at several critical moments in my life; scholarly—based on the recent advances in Old Testament research, such as form criticism, which have taught us things about Habakkuk which cannot be read in older books; and pastoral—acknowledging the continuing existence among believers in our time of the same problems which concerned Habakkuk: questions about why the righteous suffer and about the goodness and power of God.

Let me explain each of the reasons briefly. What I have called the "pastoral" importance of the book is the way it speaks to some of the deepest needs of men and women who are oppressed and depressed by the ways of this world. Those who have asked, "Why, in a world governed by a good God, does wickedness so often triumph?" will find Habakkuk wrestling with the same question. Those who do not understand why they see the righteous suffering beyond anything they could be thought to deserve, while the wicked prosper, will find their bewilderment echoed in the stirring pleas of this prophet. Those who have pondered why evil should exist at all will find their questions raised for them again, and sharpened, though not answered on an intellectual level by this book.

For this is one of those places in the Bible which wrestles with the question of theodicy—the problem of whether God really rules this world with justice. It is not the only place, and we shall compare Habakkuk with other parts of the Bible in the next chapter, but it may very well be the earliest effort in the Bible to find answers to questions such as those in the preceding paragraph—questions which have troubled believers ever since. And the way it has formulated those questions along with the kinds of answers it has offered make it one of the most valuable treatments of the theodicy question which any book has ever provided. As Raymond Calkins wrote in his book, *The Modern Message of the Minor Prophets:*

> There is no Old Testament book that is able to do more for the burdened souls of men or to raise them to higher levels of hope and confidence than the brief prophecy of Habakkuk. . . . Hardly a book in the Bible is constructed on such simple and majestic lines. These three chapters stand like three august columns, side by side, each complete in itself, unparalleled in their power and appeal. . . . Search the Bible through and you will find nothing so matchless in concentrated power as these three chapters of the Book of Habakkuk. Of the outward circumstances of the prophet's life we know nothing. But here was a man with a soul sensitive to evil, yet firm in his faith in an omnipotent God. And this faith he has uttered with a force, an eloquence, a literary power which has caused his words to become a permanent part of the literature of the soul. (P. 92f.)

Yet I mentioned earlier that Habakkuk has not given us an intellectual answer to the problem of evil. His answers are existential: they teach us how we can go on living and believing in God *in spite of* certain missing answers. That, we shall see later, is the real force of the book's most famous text: "The just shall live by his faith." (2:4, KJV)

The mere fact that this verse occurs in Habakkuk might be reason enough for us to devote ourselves to the study of the whole book. It has been identified over and over again as one of the most significant thoughts in the Bible. In early Judaism the Rabbis taught that the Bible contained 613 commandments given to Moses on Mount Sinai. But, they said, other teachers had found ways to summarize the essence of these commandments: David reduced them to eleven, in Psalm 15; Isaiah to six (Isa. 33:15–16); Micah to three (Mic. 6:8); Isaiah again to two (56:1); then Amos and Habakkuk reduced them to one ("seek me and live" in Amos 5:4, and "the just shall live by faith" in Hab. 2:4). We cannot help comparing the similar activity of Jesus in summing up the whole law in the two-fold law of love—for God and for one's neighbor (quoting Deut. 6:5 and Lev. 19:18; Matt. 22:34–40).

Jesus did not cite Habakkuk in summing up the Gospel, but Paul did. This verse became the keystone of Paul's theology, quoted by him in Romans 1:17 as a way of stating the major theme of that great work, and again in Galatians 3:12. It is quoted a third time in the New Testament, used in a different way, in Hebrews 10:36–39. As a later consequence of Paul's use of the verse it became a rallying cry of both Lutheran and Reformed theology. But now we shall look at it anew in its original setting, and when we do so we shall find that Habakkuk has something of his own to teach us about the meaning of faith.

* * * *

Modern Old Testament scholarship has paid dividends of two kinds which make a new study of Habakkuk worthwhile.

First, advances in scholarship help us to understand the book better and to hear a message of importance from verses which had previously meant very little. It has helped us to know more certainly what some of the words themselves meant, to translate certain sentences more accurately, to be able to understand the concerns and insights of the book against its setting in the life of ancient Israel, and to know something more about the prophet himself. All of this we would expect from scholarship. But Habakkuk is in some respects a special case in that although it is a *prophetic* book it has been found to be closely related to other kinds of Old Testament books. Most of the book is very much like the Psalms, the poetry of worship in the Jerusalem temple. But much of the vocabulary and many of the leading ideas of the book have their closest parallels not in prophecy or the Psalms but in the wisdom literature: Proverbs, Job and Ecclesiastes. And so we shall find that to study this book does not merely increase our understanding of three short chapters of the Old Testament, but that in fact it opens new insights into three important aspects of the life of ancient Israel: prophecy, worship, and wisdom.

As an introductory sample of such results let us see whether we can learn anything more about the author of the book than has been known in the past. A Bible dictionary will tell you very little about him; his name appears in the Old Testament only in Habakkuk 1:1 and 3:1, without any biographical information save the title, "the prophet." He also appears in the apocryphal addition to Daniel called Bel and the Dragon:

> Now the prophet Habakkuk was in Judea. He had boiled pottage and had broken bread into a bowl, and was going into the field to take it to the reapers. But the angel of the Lord said to Habakkuk, "Take the dinner which you have to Babylon, to Daniel, in the lion's den." Habakkuk said, "Sir, I have never seen Babylon, and I know nothing about the den." Then the angel of the Lord took him by the crown of his head, and lifted him by his hair and set him down in Babylon, right over the den, with the rushing sound

of the wind itself. Then Habakkuk shouted, "Daniel! Daniel! Take the dinner which God has sent you." And Daniel said, "Thou hast remembered me, O God, and hast not forsaken those who love thee." So Daniel arose and ate. And the angel of God immediately returned Habakkuk to his own place. (vss. 33–39)

This incident is obviously purely legendary. So the question facing us is whether scholarly detective work can deduce anything further about a man who clearly was one of the great thinkers of antiquity, but who is otherwise almost completely unknown.

We begin with his name. Aside from being the easiest name in the Bible to spell (you use an H-and-an-A-and-a-B-and-an-A-and-a-K-and-a-K-and-a-U-and-a-K), can it tell us anything about the man who bore it? The effort used to be made to derive it from the Hebrew root meaning "to embrace," but the form of the name is quite unusual for Hebrew. Recently the word has been found in the Akkadian language, in texts from Mesopotamia which indicate that it was the name of some garden plant. So it seems that our prophet may have borne a foreign name. Does that mean anything? We know that the civilizations of Assyria and Babylonia had a profound influence on the Israelites during this period. Perhaps that accounts for his parents' choice of the word as a name for their son. Or could he have been a foreigner who had converted to the worship of Yahweh, or (a bit more likely) the child of a mixed marriage, Israelite and Assyrian? We have no way of giving a certain answer to those questions but the very name the man bore suggests there is something unusual about him.

Next we look at his title, "the prophet" (1:1, Hebrew—*nabi'*), and discover that it is not so ordinary as we might think. In the titles to other prophetic books we find various items of information given: sometimes the name of the prophet's father (Isa. 1:1), sometimes the names of the kings contemporary with the prophet (Hos. 1:1), sometimes his home town (Amos 1:1). But only three times is the individual designated as "the prophet" in the title of his book. The two other cases are the post-exilic books Haggai and Zechariah. Now the question arises, is there anything special about that? And it is raised in our minds largely because of the intensive scholarly work which has been done on prophecy in recent years. One thing which has become clear is that there was a class of *professional* prophets in Israel, some of whom worked for the king, to advise him of God's will in political and personal affairs; while others were associated with the temple and participated in the service of worship there. When Amos said, "I am no prophet, nor a prophet's son" (Amos 7:14), he was not denying that he himself prophesied, for he went on to say immediately, "And the LORD took me from following the flock, and the LORD said to me, 'Go, prophesy to my people Israel.'" (7:15) Rather he seems to have been saying that he held amateur status as a prophet; his profession was herdsman and trimmer of sycamore trees and he did not belong to a prophetic guild (which is what is meant by "sons of the prophets," cf. 2 Kings 2:15, 4:1, 6:1). Now, sometimes we have been tempted to think that all the professional prophets are to be condemned as false prophets, because of texts such as 1 Kings 22, where the prophets who work for Ahab obviously preach whatever they think the king will like. But that is jumping to conclusions; Nathan, e.g., was attached to David's court and was no false prophet (2 Sam. 7, 12). And it may be that some of the authors of our canonical books of prophecy were professionals. The fact that Habakkuk is given the title "the prophet," while by no means conclusive, does correlate with other evidence which suggests that we can determine his occupation and location; that he was employed in the Jerusalem temple as a prophet who composed oracles and songs for the service of worship there.

That conclusion gets a bit ahead of the evidence, most of which comes from form criticism. This method of studying the Old Testament has revealed that, as in modern English, the kinds of language used by the sportscaster, the preacher, the congressman, and the disc jockey are clearly different, each one having his own style, vocabulary, and speech patterns so that each distinctive type of language can be connected with a different situation in life, so the Old Testament's language also can be analyzed and identified with various situations in the life of ancient Israel. Now, although Habakkuk is specifically called a prophet, form criticism has shown (as mentioned earlier) that his book is more closely related, as a type of literature, to Psalms and Wisdom. And form criticism will not permit us to dismiss that as unimportant; it demands to know why. The psalms were the literature of worship, used in the temple service at Jerusalem; the form criticism of the Psalter taught us that. Wisdom belonged in the royal court (advisers to the king were known as "wise men," cf. Daniel 2:12, 4:18) and in the school (wise men were also teachers, no doubt of the royal children in the early days, cf. Proverbs 1:2–6). But there are certain psalms which contain the language and ideas of the wise men very prominently (e.g., Psalms 1, 37, 119), so we can see that the court and the temple were closely related, that some of the wise men composed songs, and that the psalmists had learned much from the wise men.

The language of the book of Habakkuk suggests that this is the milieu in which he belongs—not a teacher or a singer by profession but a prophet; that is, by inspiration he receives messages from God for the edification of those who come to the temple to worship. But he is so strongly influenced by the language and ideas of those around him, the singers and teachers, that his book is more like their work than like the work of a prophet. And the reason for that is not hard to find. It is because his central concern is one which was already appearing in the work of the wise men, as affirmations of God's justice, and in the songs of worship, as laments over the suffering of the righteous. So it was natural for this prophet to take of their language to make his own distinctive contribution to the problem.

It is not hard for us, either, to understand why the questions of God's justice and the suffering of the righteous dominate Habakkuk's work, when we know something about the times during which he lived. There is only one clue in the book as to its date and that is the mention of the Chaldeans in 1:6. Although the Chaldeans occupied parts of Babylonia for a long time, the logical deduction from Habakkuk's reference is that he wrote during the time when the great Chaldean king, Nebuchadnezzar, was threatening the freedom of Judah, i.e., late in the seventh or early in the sixth century. This date has been confirmed by linguistic studies which have compared the Hebrew of Habakkuk with that of other works composed in this period and have shown that in the history of the development of the Hebrew language, Habakkuk fits best at this time, i.e., sometime near 600 B.C.

This means that Habakkuk lived in a dying nation. In 600 B.C. the little kingdom of Judah had thirteen more years to live, and the death pangs had already set in. Judah was a captive nation and had been for many years, barely hanging on to its existence and identity by paying a yearly, heavy tribute to Assyria, its overlord. For a few years, probably just about the time of Habakkuk's youth, a glimmer of hope had appeared on the international scene. The Chaldeans, who lived in the vicinity of Babylon in south Mesopotamia, became strong enough to challenge the power of mighty Assyria and with the help of the Medes from the mountains to the northeast they attacked again and again until finally that enormous empire crumbled and fell. Judah, far to the west, on the very borders of the old empire, then had a few moments to breathe, a few years without tribute while the Medes and the Chaldeans were delivering the final blows, had time to nourish new hopes of becoming an independent nation again under their able king, Josiah. But that was a vain hope, for soon Egypt moved into the power vacuum left by Assyria's demise and briefly took control of Judah until the great Nebuchadnezzar came to power in Babylonia and was able to devote his attentions to the west. By 597 B.C. he had added Judah to his empire. Ten more years of life were left to captive Judah, ruled by a vassal king,

Zedekiah, one of their own but a servant of Nebuchadnezzar and ruling by his pleasure; and then came revolt and death.

Habakkuk's book was produced in the midst of all that. When we read it with the turmoil, terror, and tragedy of those years in mind we shall see that it is a response to such a time, but, as we shall also see later, the prophet chose a way of speaking which would give his words a universal appeal so that they might speak with a peculiar directness time after time to those of other ages and places who find themselves in deep trouble.

* * * *

That brings me to the third reason, a kind of personal compulsion to write and to share my thoughts about Habakkuk which is certainly due to the value of the book itself as study has opened it to me, but is also partly the result of some remarkable coincidences between the book and several traumatic events in my life. Feeling that the autobiographical element is not completely unimportant to the work of an interpreter of Scripture, I ask your indulgence to allow me to include a bit of that here.

When I was in seminary, most of us held student pastorates in addition to carrying on our academic work. One fall, early in November, one of my fellow students asked our Old Testament professor, Dr. Mihelic, if he could recommend a good text for a Thanksgiving sermon. Dr. Mihelic said, "Yes, I'll give you a text. Turn to the last chapter of Habakkuk, verses 17 and 18." And he read:

> Though the fig tree do not blossom,
>   nor fruit be on the vines,
> the produce of the olive fail
>   and the fields yield no food,
> the flock be cut off from the fold
>   and there be no herd in the stalls,
> yet I will rejoice in the LORD,
>   I will joy in the God of my salvation.

"Now," he said, "instead of preaching from something like the Psalms which thank God for his abundant good gifts, why don't you, for once, think about those who don't live with abundance and yet thank God all the same?"

Well, I filed that suggestion mentally, for possible future use. Frankly, I didn't know quite what to make of it at the time. But, a couple of years later it came to mind as I began to plan my preaching for Thanksgiving time. I had begun graduate work at the University of Chicago and at the same time continued to serve the church in eastern Iowa where I had worked during seminary days. And one Monday morning in mid-November as I rode the train to Chicago I read the book of Habakkuk. "When can you preach such a text?" I thought. Will it make any sense to people who are healthy, secure, and comfortable? Or is that exactly when they need it? Would it seem a mockery to people in distress to be told they ought to rejoice?

I still hadn't decided, when the train reached Chicago, whether I could preach on that text or not. But when I reached my room at the university there was word of a telephone call from one of the elders in my church. He had called to tell me that the young woman in the church whom I had been dating (and who is now my wife) had been critically injured in a head-on collision that morning. I took the next train back, not knowing whether she would be alive when I reached her, and on that return ride I read the book of Habakkuk again. It meant something different to me then. During the week that followed I found that my distress was shared by everyone in the little community where we lived, for not only had my future wife been seriously injured, but the man whose car collided with hers, a young father who lived on the same street, had been killed instantly. Two weeks later I preached a Thanksgiving sermon from Habakkuk, and it seemed to make sense to us.

A year later we were married and two months after that my mother and father were killed instantly in a head-on collision. As their minister talked to me about the funeral service he told me that the night before their death my parents had attended a Lenten study group in which the subject had been that verse from Habakkuk which is quoted three times in the New Testament, "The just shall live by his faith," and the minister said he would like to take that verse as the text for his funeral sermon, since it fit their lives so well. And that is what he preached.

Again I turned to the book of Habakkuk to read and to ponder, and periodically since then I have felt it both an obligation and a reward to attempt to understand more fully this brief though magnificent work. Most recently President William Jackson of Winebrenner Theological Seminary kindly invited me to lecture to the annual conference of ministers of the Church of God in North America at Findlay, Ohio, and was willing to indulge my desire to take Habakkuk as the subject. This book is based to a considerable extent on those lectures and is the result of President Jackson's kindness at the end, Professor Mihelic's inspiration at the beginning, and that combination of circumstances which I have outlined, in between.

* * * *

Habakkuk's book divides neatly into three sections and we shall devote a chapter to each. Chapter II will deal with Habakkuk 1:2—2:4, the dialogue between God and the prophet on the subject of God's justice. Chapter III will take up the meaning of the woe-oracles in Habakkuk 2:5–20, and Chapter IV will discuss the psalm which is contained in Habakkuk 3.

BUT THE JUST SHALL LIVE BY HIS FAITH

Habakkuk's task is God Himself, the effort to find what He means by permitting tyranny and wrong.

—George Adam Smith

Habakkuk begins with the cry of an anguished human being who sees suffering and injustice all around him and who cannot reconcile this with what he has been taught about the righteousness and power of his God. And so, like thousands of others, some of whom we ourselves know, he asks God, "Why?" The questioning, the pleading, the accusations are not unusual—they are known to all of us—but something unusual follows them. Habakkuk claims that God answered him. We have already noted that in many respects his work is more like that of a wise man or psalmist than a prophet, but here he does make the claim which all prophets make, that God spoke to him. Furthermore, the structure of this first section of his book takes the form of a dialogue; twice the prophet complains and twice God answers him.

Now, we may well believe that God has answered prayers for us, and we have heard others claim that God has spoken to them, but still there is something unusual about this conversation. Most people, even in the Bible, who have longed for the privilege of arguing with God, of questioning the way he does things, of seeking God's own explanation of his ways, have not been given that opportunity. Remember Job, who asked for it over and over, demanding that God give an account of himself, but God refused to do it. What Habakkuk has recorded here is something rather extraordinary: a dialogue in which he twice complains to God about the world's injustice, and twice God answers him.

What are we to make of this? In our day, the natural response of many may be to think of this dialogue as an imaginary one, created in the mind of the author. But without going into the psychology of inspiration or the question of the forms in which a human being might receive a message from God, I believe it is possible to affirm that there were "inspired persons" in ancient Israel who in some way "heard" the word of God. Certainly it is unusual for a prophet to record such a conversation between himself and God, but we can find a few other examples of this which we shall compare later, and my conclusion is that this section of our book, unusual though it may be, ought to be heard by us as an authentic record of a dialogue between man and God concerning God's justice.

But that does not make this so completely beyond the realm of the experience and comprehension of most of us as it might seem. I am not suggesting that Habakkuk was somehow transported into heavenly realms, in the manner reported by mystics, to participate in a relationship with God which is denied to others, for he does not create a brand-new language to express himself as he reports this experience. He uses the traditional language which Israel used in its worship and so, despite the unusual aspects of the dialogue, it remains very much on the level where his fellow Israelites lived. I believe that if we begin our reflections on this passage with a consideration of where Habakkuk got the language he used it will speak all the more directly to us, for although we are not ancient Israelites there is much that we have in common with their faith and their problems.

Although there are no quotation marks in the original Hebrew and there is only one explicit introduction of a speaker in the passage (2:2), by reading carefully we can discern four major divisions in it: a complaint uttered by the prophet in 1:2–4, a message from God in 1:5–11, a further complaint in 1:12–17, a brief statement by the prophet of what he intends to do in 2:1 and another divine speech in 2:2–4. So the structure is clear and easy to outline. The one problem is in deciding whether 2:5 is the concluding verse of this first major portion of the book or whether it belongs with 2:6–20 as the initial verse of the second section. We shall have to look at that problem a little later.

If we now return to the question of where the language of each of the subdivisions of our section came from, we can begin to trace in the scenery and the cast of the drama of which Habakkuk now remains the lone speaker. Here is where form criticism again is a help to us, for we find that 1:2–4 is in language and subject matter a psalm very similar to a large number of those in the Psalter which the form critics call *psalms of lament.* In these songs the singer comes to God to complain about his troubles and the troubles of his people. (Some are strongly individual in emphasis, such as Psalm 13, while others are strongly communal, e.g. Psalm 74.) He reminds God of his reputation for justice and of the promises he has made to his people (this we find in Habakkuk's second complaint, vss. 12–13), then he describes the injustice that is rampant in the world and asks, Why? and, How long? So, when Habakkuk assails us and God at the very beginning with,

> O LORD, how long shall I cry for help,
>   and thou wilt not hear?
> Or cry to thee "Violence!"
>   and thou wilt not save?   (VS. 2)

we understand that he is echoing the pleas of the psalmists who wrote:

> How long, O LORD? Wilt thou forget me for ever? . . .
>   . . .
> How long must I bear pain in my soul,
>   and have sorrow in my heart all the day?
> How long shall my enemy be exalted over me?
>   (PS. 13:1–2)
>
> How long, O God, is the foe to scoff?
> Is the enemy to revile thy name for ever?   (PS. 74:10)

> How long, O LORD? Wilt thou hide thyself for ever?
> How long will thy wrath burn like fire?   (PS. 89:46)

And when he appeals for an explanation,

> Why dost thou make me see wrongs   (VS. 3A)
>   and look upon trouble?

he is in company with those psalmists who plead for answers which do not come:

> Why art thou so far from helping me . . .
> I cry by day but thou dost not answer,
>   and by night, but find no rest.   (PS. 22:1B,2)

So this impassioned language is not something born afresh from the anguish of Habakkuk's soul; as he cried for help (vs. 2) so did the authors of Psalms such as 22 (just quoted) and 88, to cite but two examples:

> O LORD, my God, I call for help by day;
>   I cry out in the night before thee . . .
> But I, O LORD, cry to thee,
>   in the morning my prayer comes before thee.
>   (PS. 88:1, 13)

From these parallels (and others which could be added) we learn that it was not a peculiar problem of the man Habakkuk which led him to utter these words, that it was no unique situation calling for a unique formulation, for he used the traditional language of worship of the people Israel. The Psalms teach us that part of Israel's worship involved the making of these impassioned pleas to God for help in times of desperate trouble. I want to say a good deal more about this later; let it suffice for now to emphasize that Israel complained about its troubles, about the injustices of life not in letters to the editor (if they had had such things) or in the local tavern, but in worship, in the presence of God himself in the sanctuary. It is clear why they did that. They brought these pleas to God because they fervently believed that he is good and just, that he cared for them and intended to help them. And it was because they believed this so strongly that they became so disturbed and their language became so violent when to all appearances God did not hear or answer.

But we must move on, for the present, for what comes next in this book does have the appearance of being an answer.

Verses 5–11 are an oracle, a word from God, as we learn from 5b and 6 which describe things only God could claim to do, and so we would expect it to be the answer to the prophet's complaint. Form criticism would classify this as a *prophecy of judgment* of the kind that appears often in the prophetic books. God announces that he is raising up a foreign nation to use its armies as an instrument of punishment against those who have disobeyed him. In this case it is the Chaldeans and it is important to note that all the emphasis is on the terror produced by their coming. Elsewhere in the prophets we encounter similar threats:

> "For behold, I will raise up against you a nation,
>> O house of Israel," says the LORD, the God of hosts;
> "and they shall oppress you from the entrance of Hamath
>> to the Brook of the Arabah."   (AMOS 6:14)

> "Behold I am bringing upon you a nation from afar,
>> O house of Israel."   (JER. 5:15)

> "Ah, Assyria, the rod of my anger,
>> the staff of my fury!
> Against a godless nation I send him,
>> and against the people of my wrath I command him."
>>   (ISA. 10:5, 6A)

In other texts of the Old Testament, then, when God speaks in the way he has done in Habakkuk 1:5–11 it is not in answer to someone's prayer for help but is a terrible threat of divine judgment against a disobedient people. What kind of answer to Habakkuk is that? This is an important question for us, but we cannot try to answer it yet, for this is a subject to which we must return after we have surveyed each part of the dialogue.

Now we encounter again the language of the psalms of lament, in vss. 12–17. Here, however, some additional features of those psalms are introduced which did not appear in vss. 2–4. A typical method used by the psalmist as he pleaded with God for help was to appeal to what he believed to be God's true character as if he were reminding God that things are not going as they should in a world ruled by divine providence:

> For thou art not a God who delights in wickedness;
> > evil may not sojourn with thee.
> The boastful may not stand before thy eyes;
> > thou hatest all evildoers.
> Thou destroyest those who speak lies;
> > the LORD abhors bloodthirsty and deceitful men.
>
> > > > > > (PS. 5:4, 5)

So Habakkuk begins his second lament with a confession of faith in the true nature of God:

> Art thou not from everlasting,
> > O LORD my God, my Holy One?
> We shall not die.   (VS. 12A)

Habakkuk continues, as the psalms of lament so often do, with an affirmation of God's goodness, put as if God needed to be reminded of that in order that he should do something about the mess the world is in:

> Thou who are of purer eyes than to behold evil
> > and canst not look on wrong,
> why dost thou look on faithless men,
> > and art silent when the wicked swallows up
> > the man more righteous than he?   (VS. 13)

Note the reappearance of the typical "Why?" question.

The rest of this complaint, vss. 14–17, is a description of the actions of the wicked in vigorous imagery, another common feature of the psalms of lament. This was apparently another means used by Israelite worshippers to motivate God to answer their pleas—by describing in detail how wicked their enemies were and how desperately they were suffering under them. We need not quote similar passages here, I think; the reader may want to consult Psalms 10:3–9, 22:16–21, 74:4–8 as good examples of this tendency.

After the prophet's statement of his intention to wait for an answer (2:1) there appears another oracle (2:2–4); the first unit in the book to have a proper introduction: "And the Lord answered me." We shall look at the contents of that oracle later, but before we end our survey of the forms and structure of the passage we ought to look again at the fact that these four speeches are arranged as a dialogue between God and man. I have said that this is somewhat unusual but not unparalleled in the Bible, and so we ought to look at the parallels which can be found.

We are not searching for any and every kind of conversation between man and God, so will leave out such things as the discussion between God and the first couple in Eden (Genesis 3) and the dialogues which occur typically in call stories (Moses, Exod. 3–4; Gideon, Judg. 6; Samuel, 1 Sam. 3; Isaiah, Isa. 6; Jeremiah, Jer. 1). We are looking for human complaints which are answered by God. One fascinating example of this is Abraham's plea on behalf of the city of Sodom in Genesis 18:23–33. Abraham's theme is stated in vss. 23 and 25: "Wilt thou indeed destroy the righteous with the wicked? . . . Shall not the Judge of all the earth do right?" It is most tempting to expound that dialogue here but we cannot do more than point out to the reader that in this passage, as we noted in the Psalms, the human demand that God ought to *act* justly is based solely on the conviction that God *is* just.

Among the numerous dialogues between Moses and God which are recorded in the Old Testament are some in which the question of what is right is at issue. We shall simply allude to Numbers 11:11–15, where Moses complains about the heavy burden of dealing with the rebellious Israelites and God responds by providing help; to Numbers 12:9–15, where God has struck Miriam with leprosy for her insubordination and Moses pleads successfully for her; and to Numbers 14:11–35, where God is about to give up on rebellious Israel and start anew but is persuaded to be patient by Moses.

Much closer parallels to our book appear in the "Confessions" of Jeremiah, and the reason for that is clear once we examine their language closely for they are also psalms of lament, followed sometimes by divine oracles. Let me cite just a few lines which will remind you of the materials from Habakkuk 1 and the psalms which were discussed earlier:

> Why does the way of the wicked prosper?
> Why do all who are treacherous thrive?   (JER. 12:1B)

> How long will the land mourn,
>   and the grass of every field wither?   (JER. 12:4A)

> Whenever I speak, I cry out,
>   I shout, "Violence and destruction!"   (JER. 20:8)

These texts cannot quite be called dialogues, but some do contain a complaint followed by an answer from God (11:18–20 with an answer in vss. 21–23; 12:1–4 answered in vss. 5–6; 15:10–18 answered in vss. 19–21). Others are merely complaints (17:9–10, 14–18; 18:18–23; 20:7–18). The kinds of answers received by Jeremiah are of some interest to us to compare and contrast with what Habakkuk heard. The first is a promise to punish those who plotted against the prophet (11:21–23), the second in effect rebukes him, saying if you complain now what will you do when the going gets rough (12:5–6), and the third puts him to the test with a conditional promise (15:19–21). None is quite like the answers given to Habakkuk, and in no case do we hear what Jeremiah's response to the answer was.

Job was mentioned in passing at the beginning of this chapter for his book is like Habakkuk in several respects. The great central section of the book (chapters 3:1—42:6) is in dialogue form, but most of it is among human beings. Job, it is true, asks for dialogue with God and complains bitterly because God doesn't respond. In the end God speaks, but that is only to have the last word, not to take up Job's questions, so although the problems raised by Job and Habakkuk are the same it appears that the kind of resolution of those problems which is offered is somewhat different.

A few Psalms quote the word from God which has been received in answer to their requests. These are very direct and positive answers (Pss. 12:5, 60:6–8), in contrast to the type of response we have been finding in Jeremiah, Job, and Habakkuk.

Finally we may note that the structure of the apocryphal book I Baruch is that of lament followed by confession of sins, and then an answer is given to the lament using prophetic and wisdom terminology. These partial parallels to the structure of Habakkuk 1:2—2:4 teach us that there must have been a common tradition in Israel of wrestling with God over the hard questions of life, that these wrestlings were not restricted to the privacy of one's own head or close circle of friends, but that they were a part of public worship in their original form (as the large number of Psalms of lament—about one third of the 150—reveals), and that this language of worship was also taken over into other kinds of texts in order to express some of the deepest concerns of prophets and wise men. The prevalence of this kind of intellectual activity and the vigor with which it was conducted also teaches us that when Israel came to God with a question they expected, nay, demanded, an answer.

* * * *

Before taking up the subject of this first section of Habakkuk for deeper consideration, since I shall not be offering a verse-by-verse treatment of the passage I should like to ask you to read it through again in my translation, with a few annotations:

[The prophet speaks:]

How long, Lord, have I cried for help,   (2)
    and you do not listen?
I shout to you, 'Violence!'
    and you do not help!
Why do you let me see trouble   (3)
    and bear with misfortune?
Despoliation and violence are before me;
    there is contention, and strife arises.
So law is powerless   (4)
    and justice never comes;
For the wicked circumvents the righteous,
    so that justice comes out perverted.

[God's message:]

Look among the nations and see,   (5)
    stare in astonishment and be astounded;
For a deed is being done in your days
    which you would not believe if it were told.
For behold, I am raising up the Chaldeans,   (6)
    that bitter and headstrong nation
    which advances to the far regions of the earth
        to occupy dwellings not its own.
Terrible and frightful is he,   (7)
    he makes his own justice and dignity.
Swifter than leopards are his horses,   (8)
    and sharper than the desert wolves.
His steeds paw the ground,
    his steeds come from afar;
They fly like the vulture
    eager for food.
All of it comes for violence   (9)
    his face strains forward,
    and he gathers up captives like sand.
He makes a mockery of kings,   (10)
    and viziers are a joke to him.
He laughs at every fortress,

for he piles up dirt and takes it.
Then the wind changes and he passes on; (11)
    guilty, he who makes of his power his god.
[The prophet's complaint continues:]
Are you not from the beginning, Lord, (12)
    My God, my Holy One, Undying?
    [or: My God, my Holy One, we shall not die.]
O Lord, is it for justice you established him?
    O Rock, for reproof did you appoint him?
Too pure of eye to look upon evil, (13)
    you cannot countenance misfortune
—then *why* do you countenance treachery,
    and be silent when the wicked swallows
        one more righteous than he?
You make man like the fish of the sea, (14)
    like the creeping thing which has no master.
[and the fisherman, who catches such creatures, is like the
        Chaldean]
He brings everything up by his fishhook, (15)
    he drags it away in his net
    and gathers it in his seine;
        so he laughs and rejoices.
Thus he sacrifices to his net (16)
    and burns incense to his seine.
For in them is his choice portion
    and his food is succulent.
Is he thus to go on emptying his net (17)
    by killing nations without compassion?
[His complaint ended, the prophet reveals his intentions: (2:1)]
Let me stand upon my watchtower,
    that I may be on guard upon the bulwark;
And I will watch to see what he will say to me
    and what return he will make to my complaint.
Then the Lord answered me and said: (2)
Write the vision
    and engrave it upon tablets,

So that one may read it running.

For again the vision is for an appointed time   (3)
    and it hastens to the end
      and will not lie;
If it lingers, wait for it,
    for it is certainly coming,
      it will not delay.

Behold the presumptuous one, his life is unstable,   (4)
    but the righteous shall live by his faithfulness.

* * * *

The single subject of this first section of Habakkuk's book is theodicy, the problem of God's justice. It is a familiar problem to all of us from our study of the Bible and from the daily experiences of ourselves and those around us. Why does evil seem to run rampant in a world which we believe was created and is ruled by a good God? Why do the righteous so often suffer while the wicked flourish and live in prosperity? Most often we hear the issue raised in more personal terms. Why has this happened to me? What have I done to deserve this? Why doesn't God do something? And sometimes only the description of a tragedy, followed by "It just makes you wonder," but we know what they're wondering about. I need not dwell on the kinds of events which raise those questions for us; they are all too familiar. But I believe it may be helpful, before we look again at Habakkuk's dialogue with God, to think about the presuppositions which the prophet held, and which we share, which are actually responsible for creating the problem. These are certain beliefs about God and about the nature of evil which are shared by every Old Testament writer and most of us have inherited them and affirm them to be true. However, if one denies the truth of any of them, the problem of evil in every one of the manifold forms in which it has been posed in Judaism and Christianity quickly disappears. And since the existence of evil in a world supposedly created and ruled by a good God lies at the heart of the theodicy question, it is important to recognize what these three essential presuppositions are.

Omnipotence. Behind Habakkuk's problem lies the assumption that there is only one God who does not share his power with any other. He made the whole world and everything in it and he is sovereign over it. How then could there be anything in it which is not the result of his will? To deny the truth of that assumption would rather effectively solve our problem. If, as in polytheistic religions, there are many gods, some can be thought to be good and responsible for all in the world that is good, while others can be given an evil character and made responsible for the world's evil. But the Bible claims there is but one God, one source of all things, and so the Bible has a problem with evil.

Righteousness. The God of Habakkuk is not unconcerned with what goes on in the world he made, nor is he wicked in his dealings with it. He loves his creatures, he is just in his dealings with them and he insists that they deal justly with one another. Usually justice is thought to mean reward for good deeds and punishment for sins, but even if a righteous person is willing to give up any claim to reward, as Habakkuk does later and as Jesus taught (Luke 17:7–10), that does not resolve the problem of injustice. There exists in this world what appears to be completely unnecessary cruelty, wholly gratuitous suffering, and that must somehow be reconciled with our belief in a just God quite apart from any concern about reward and punishment. We have seen how Habakkuk in 1:13 asserts his conviction that God is "of purer eyes than to behold evil," but if God is omnipotent and righteous how has evil come to be and how can it continue? Once again the problem can be eliminated by denying the righteousness of God, asserting that he is evil by nature or, more likely, that God simply does not care. But the Bible refuses to take either of these ways out of the dilemma.

The reality of evil. "If God is good and God is all, therefore all is good and evil does not really exist." So reasoned Mary Baker

Eddy, the founder of Christian Science. But the Bible never reasoned that way. It insists that evil is not merely an appearance, illusion or delusion; it is horribly real. It cannot be denied or wished away but must be dealt with in life, and eventually must be tackled on an intellectual level if what we say we believe is to make any sense at all. The dilemma has been partially resolved in a variety of ways in Judaism and Christianity, but since this is not a book on the problem of evil I think it is best to restrict ourselves to the way in which the problem surfaces in the book of Habakkuk and to the ways in which he deals with it. But we may do so with the certainty that his three presuppositions are firmly held, and that if he finds any kind of resolution to his problem it will be one which does not deny the truth of any of them.

The Dilemma

Habakkuk's book begins abruptly, with no hint of what has gone wrong or in what situation the prophet is raising the complaint. We tried to fill in some of that background in the first chapter, but here we are simply struck with an attack directed against God himself. "You do not listen—You do not save—You make me see wrongs, and look on trouble." The reasons for this violent attack are made explicit; it is as a character in *Green Pastures* said: "Everything that's fastened down is coming loose." Justice is perverted; the wicked outwit the righteous, and God does not save.

Wilhelm Vischer said in his essay on Habakkuk that this kind of talk is startling to those who do not know the Bible and who think that men of faith never speak to God in such a bold way. It seems to many that the way of faith is to wait in patience and silence for God's redemption from trouble, but in the Scriptures we find that it is not unbelief but the strength of one's faith that forces one to ask of God impatiently, "How long?" and the reason for this is that God has made it so. It is he who has taught us that his way is a way of justice and righteousness. It is he who has promised us redemption. It is his word that makes us hunger and thirst after righteousness. So if we truly believe the Gospel which has taught us that God is sovereign and righteous, and our Savior, then we *must* ask, "Why?" and, "How long?" As Abraham Heschel has written in his book, *Man Is Not Alone*, "If we possess the vision of justice, it must eminently be in God. Even the cry of despair: There is no justice in heaven!—is a cry in the name of justice, a justice that cannot have come out of us and still be missing in the source of ourselves."

Habakkuk hears the word of God in response to his attack, and we read it in vss. 5–11. And yet, as we have already seen, that is not quite the word we were expecting and hoping for. And we have begun to question whether that is any answer at all to Habakkuk's problem and ours. Now it is true that most of the commentaries you will consult suggest that there is a way to understand this as a valid answer from God to Habakkuk's protest. They will say that the prophet has been complaining about the prosperity of the wicked among his own people and that in response to that God told him he was bringing the Chaldeans from afar as his agents to punish the unrighteous. This is not an unreasonable suggestion by any means, for other prophets declared most explicitly that God uses the foreign nations in just that way. Isaiah spoke of Assyria as the rod of the Lord used to chastize a rebellious people (Isa. 10:5–6) and both Jeremiah and Ezekiel interpreted the coming of the Chaldean armies under Nebuchadnezzar in the same way (Jer. 25:8–14; Ezek. 21:18–23). As a matter of fact, Habakkuk himself refers to such an interpretation in vs. 12b:

> O LORD, thou hast ordained them as a judgment;
> and thou, O Rock, hast established them
> for chastisement,

the Revised Standard Version translates it, so one might think that settles the matter. That it does not is made clear by the abundant evidence that the answer does not satisfy Habakkuk, nor does it satisfy me, and so you will note that in my translation the sentence appears as a question, not a statement.

There is no hint in God's answer of comfort or assurance that he is with the righteous to save them. The tone throughout is intended to terrify. To be invaded by a merciless foreign army is what God promises, and that means that all will suffer, guilty and innocent alike. How can this be called justice? God says the Chaldeans are coming for *violence* (vs. 9); the very thing about which Habakkuk has been complaining, and so he seems to be warning that things are going to get worse and not better and that the Chaldeans are not the remedy for the prophet's distress.

What, then, shall we make of this answer if we are not satisfied that the traditional explanations are adequate? We have encountered one of the difficult problems of interpretation which this book poses and it is one that has puzzled scholars for a long time. One of the suggested solutions which we might consider is the proposal that the parts of this chapter have become disarranged somehow, so that rearrangements can be suggested which might recover the hypothetical original order. For example, if the threat which we have just been considering came first, then we could understand Habakkuk's complaint as a reaction to that, which would be easier to understand than taking the threat as an answer to the complaint. An additional problem is posed by the relationship between the threat in vss. 5–11 and the renewed complaint in vss. 12–17. If God predicts the coming of the Chaldeans in vss. 5–11 and Habakkuk complains they have made the situation worse in vss. 12–17 then presumably this dialogue could not have taken place all at one time and there would have to be an interval of months or years between vs. 11 and vs. 12.

I have a suggestion to make which is not wholly original and which does not finally settle the matter by any means, but which does, I believe, provide a way of dealing with the chapter which is faithful to its message.

(a) We admit that vss. 5–11 are no satisfactory answer to the complaint in vss. 2–4. Then:

(b) *either* Habakkuk complained about the injustice in the world in which he lived and God responded with the threat that the Chaldeans were coming; then at some time, either immediately or only at an interval after they had come, Habakkuk recognized that the Chaldeans had only aggravated the problem and responded with the second complaint;

(c) *or* Habakkuk first received an oracle (vss. 5–11) threatening the arrival of the Chaldeans as God's agents to punish the wicked in Judah, just as other prophets had; but for him this threat created a serious theological problem because he saw that the wickedness which already troubled him would thereby be compounded. So he directed to God a complaint composed of the entire present first chapter and as a part of the complaint *quoted* God's oracle as one of the things that had created his problem. In this case the oracle was never in any sense an answer to his dilemma but was a part of the problem from the beginning. In either case (b) or case (c) the meaning of the chapter is basically the same. All around him Habakkuk sees injustice and oppression and violence, and the word from God which he has received or does receive simply promises more of the same.

Shall we become homiletical for a moment and consider whether this has any parallels in the twentieth century? I believe that it does. We Old Testament scholars are very fond of talking about how God works in history and reveals himself through his mighty acts. But sometimes embarassing questions have been raised about how you can identify an act of God in history—how do you distinguish it from an ordinary event? I believe that in the book of Habakkuk we can discover that even the prophets of ancient Israel, who supposedly had that special gift of being able to read the divine purpose in history, found that sometimes the events of their time were opaque to them. This book does not make everything clear, does not pretend to explain exactly what God is about, as Isaiah and Jeremiah and Ezekiel did. So maybe we can feel a sort of kinship with Habakkuk which we do not sense with those other worthies, for he is one of the faithful (like some of us) who believes that God is working in history, all right, but who must acknowledge that at the present what God is doing seems incomprehensible or may even seem to be counterproductive. And, as we shall see by the time we reach the end of this section, it is what the faithful do when the vision is lacking or is downright negative in its implications that is the ultimate concern of this prophet.

But before we hasten on too quickly to the answers of chapter 2, perhaps there is something more that should be said about the dilemma of the first chapter as a true reflection of one of the mysteries of faith. Job said, "The soul of the wounded cries for help; yet God pays no attention to their prayer." (24:12) That is surely one of the most terrible statements to be found anywhere in the Bible, and yet, on the human level, isn't that the way it really seems to be, far too much of the time? We say to people in the name of the gospel, "God is good, God is just, God is love, God cares for you, God will help if you turn to him," and they *do* turn to him in prayer; they plead for help. But some still die in pain from disease, some are left widows or orphans, some lose their jobs and can't find others, some lose everything by storm or accident, some cannot fight the power of the wicked and are crushed beneath it. And what more can we say to them?

There *must* be something more, or we are without hope and might as well give up the gospel. This book says it, as we shall see in good time. But first, if we are to be of any help to those who have truly been crushed by the tragedies of life, if we are not to be mockingly cheerful, falsely optimistic Pollyannas, I believe that we must cry out, with those victims and with Job and Jeremiah and Habakkuk, Why? and How long? We want answers, and have a right to want them; we have some answers in the gospel, but to offer glib answers to the tragedies of life is not to take seriously God's word of justice and mercy.

Several years ago, after Professor Robert Spike was murdered, our seminary held a memorial service since several of our faculty members had known him well. It was a typically Christian service, strongly positive in its attitudes toward tragedy and death. But afterwards one faculty member said to me that under the circumstances he felt that there was something wrong with it, for murder had been committed and a valuable life had been wrongfully cut short. He said he strongly felt the need for some of the Old Testament language in which wickedness is cursed. Whether or not his feelings about that particular event were justified, his comments may raise valid questions about whether worship, as Christians usually practice it, really deals with all the needs of believers, and especially of the desperate.

Should there be a place in public, Christian worship for liturgies such as those in Habakkuk and the psalms of lament? Christian worship tends to be all triumph, all good news (even the confession of sin is not a very awesome experience because we know the assurance of pardon is coming; it's printed in the bulletin). And what does that say to those who, at the moment, know nothing of triumph? That they've muffed it, somehow? That their faith hasn't been strong enough to grant them success? That the whole business is a fraud?

We hope not. But has the Christian gospel completely eliminated the need, which Israel recognized so clearly, to lay all the failures of this life very openly before God himself and ask him, as a believing, worshiping community, Why and how long? I think perhaps it has not, although I recognize that to many Christians life on this side of the cross is believed to have eliminated the legitimacy of such questions. Yet pain and oppression and injustice are still with us and it is not enough just to say to one suffering the present hurt of all that, "Christ is the answer." We need to cry with them first and plead with God a bit. "Smile, God loves you," is too little to offer, but most of our corporate worship, I fear, does not move beyond that level.

Perseverance

I spoke earlier of taking God's word of justice and mercy seriously. How to do that is the subject of the opening words of chapter 2. We are told that the way of faith is perseverance, insisting that there must be an answer, refusing to give up on the truth of what we believe about God, refusing to give way to cynicism or unbelief. I need not dwell on the symbol of the watchtower; it is a well-chosen image to represent persistence in seeking and waiting for God's word, and needs no explanation. Jesus created another picturesque depiction of perseverance which it is well to recall here, in his parable of the importunate widow (Luke 18:1–8). Luke's introduction to the parable says that he told it "to the effect that they ought always to pray and not lose heart." Some of the language of the parable is reminiscent of the laments we have been reading in the Old Testament. The widow kept coming to the unjust judge and saying, "vindicate me against my adversary," the kind of thing addressed to God in Pss. 7:1,6; 17:1–2, 13–14; 27:12; 31:15; 35:29, etc. But he, in a way like God in our Old Testament texts, did not respond until finally, just to rid himself of her nuisance (unlike God's motivation for answering our prayers), he agreed to deal with her case. Jesus' conclusion is that if even an unrighteous judge will finally vindicate the persistent, how much more will it be true that God will "vindicate his elect, who cry to him day and night."

It has been said that often those who question God's justice are to a great extent indulging in self-pity. That may be true in many cases and we need to beware of falling into that trap, yet that possibility ought not to keep us from any and all serious questionings of God. The danger lurking on the other side is that we become guilty of that "weak resignation to the evils we deplore" of which Harry Emerson Fosdick wrote in his hymn, "God of Grace and God of Glory." And that weak resignation has been known to masquerade under the name of faith.

George Adam Smith was correct, I believe, in picking this point in his commentary on Habakkuk to talk about scepticism. Sometimes men such as Job and Ecclesiastes have been called the skeptics of the Old Testament because of the way they have challenged the orthodoxy of their day, and if that is an appropriate label for them, it could be applied to Habakkuk as well. But if we use the word "skeptic" of these men we must make it clear that it means they are "questioners," not men without faith. For most people, skepticism, doubt of any kind, connotes unbelief, and this has led many a faithful Christian to fear questions, to be unwilling to bring to light the unresolved issues that lie somewhere inside and to bring them to God asking help in finding the truth. But I say skepticism is not to be feared, for as Smith wrote, the attitude of the greatest skeptics is not only one of earnestness and sincerity, but of recognition of *duty towards the truth*. They do not give up and say there is no truth, or the truth can never be found; rather like Habakkuk they climb to the watchtower to strain every level of their intellects in the search for truth. The presence of those great questioners in the Bible, Job, Habakkuk, Ecclesiastes—Jeremiah also—ought to teach us that God is by no means displeased with those who question him. Indeed, perhaps we reveal the depth of our faith that God really does intend to keep his promises, when we come to him to ask him how long it will be before we see the fulfillment.

God's answer to Habakkuk, we hear in 2:2–3, is commendation for such an attitude and encouragement for those who persevere.

Faithfulness

Yet we may still wonder whether we have an answer when we read vss. 2–4 of chapter 2, for it is still not quite what Habakkuk had asked for or what we had expected. In a little essay on this prophet, D. M. Lloyd-Jones remarked that God's answers are *usually* different from what we expect, and that probably comes very near to being a general truth. But if it be asked whether vss. 2–4 are any answer at all, I am prepared to say that for those who can accept it as God's kind of answer (rather than our own kind) it is answer enough.

Verses 2–3 are a response to the How long? question. God recognizes that those who ask the question may be tempted to supply their own answer, and that it will be *forever*. It is to that danger, to the possibility of losing faith, of giving up and no longer expecting anything of God, that God speaks. "It will surely come, it will not delay." And yet his words seem to contradict themselves; it is hastening but it awaits its time! It will not delay but it seems slow and we must wait for it! In these, at first puzzling words, is to be found God's way of assuring us that there is indeed an answer and that he *will* give it; that he will act on behalf of his people and does not forsake them—but that this can come only in his own good time. At this point we are frankly left with a mystery, because we cannot calculate the time, we do not understand why the time is not Now. Only God knows that. And that is where faith comes in.

"But the just shall live by his faith." This is the familiar form of vs. 4b as the King James Version translated it. This sentence is just three words in Hebrew; words formed from three powerful roots: righteous, faith, and live. More exactly the middle one is "faithfulness," and so the modern translations render it. Each of the three words deserves careful attention before we attempt to conclude what the sentence meant to Habakkuk.

The *just* (Hebrew, *tsaddîk*), the righteous one, is the one who has been vindicated, whom God has declared to be right. There is a legal background to this word; it denotes the winner in a case at law in some of its Old Testament uses. So it is not restricted in its reference to a purely internal quality of goodness which one may possess. It is used in situations of controversy to denote the side which is right. Its opposite is wicked (Hebrew, *rasha'*), and we saw the two words paired in 1:4 and 1:13.

God himself is righteous (cf. Jeremiah's use of the word in one of his confessions, 12:1) and those human beings whom he declares to be righteous are those who please him in all ways. Now, since the word so often is used in a situation of controversy and contrast, to denote those whom God favors, it seems likely that the first line of vs. 4, which is so difficult to translate, represents the other side of the issue. The word "wicked" does not appear this time; instead we have a word which should be an opposite to "righteous" but which occurs only in this one place in the Old Testament, so that we are not completely certain of its meaning. The King James Version reads:

Behold, his soul which is lifted up is not upright in him.

The Revised Standard Version resorts to a conjecture:

Behold, he whose soul is not upright in him shall fail,

and points out in a footnote that the Hebrew word translated "lifted up" in the KJV really means "puffed up." The conjecture which the RSV adopted is one which many scholars have suggested; it merely involves assuming that a scribe in antiquity copying the text of Habakkuk transposed two of the letters of the puzzling word, and if so the original word would have been one which means "to be weak, to collapse, to succumb, to fail." But if we take the word to be an opposite of "just," as I have suggested, then its present form may perhaps be the original one and it may be taken to mean something like "heedless," as one possibility, or "puffed up," probably in the sense of "presumptuous." But we must confess that these are guesses, and any decision about what the verse means must work around this uncertain word.

To *live* is not merely to exist, in Hebrew thought. One is not really alive when sick, weak, in danger or with a damaged reputation. To be *alive* is to have vigor, security and honor. So this verse does not merely tell us how we can barely hang on to some feeble thread of existence in times such as Habakkuk describes; no, it speaks of being richly and fully alive. That interpretation is confirmed by 3:17–18. The opposite of it is to be found in vs. 4a, in words which are not easy to translate either, but which mean something like:

> his soul is not true in him,
> or, his life is not straight in him.
> or, his personality is not upright in him.

There are other possibilities, but the intended contrast seems to be between life and the distortion or perversion of human existence, and so earlier I translated it, "his life is unstable."

Now we come to *faith* and *faithfulness*, for the two concepts cannot be separated. The Hebrew word *('emunah)* sometimes means "to be steadfast"; when the Israelites were battling the Amalekites in the wilderness and found that they were successful as long as they could see Moses' upraised arms, Aaron and Hur helped by holding his arms *steady* (Exod. 17:12). It can mean to discharge a public office faithfully (2 Chron. 19:9) or to be faithful in marriage (Hosea 2:20). It can mean truth in speech and in testimony (Proverbs 12:17, 14:5). Seldom in the Old Testament does it denote "faith" in the sense of what one believes (Isa. 7:9b). But that does not mean that Paul was wrong in taking Habakkuk 2:4 as the great theme verse for his teaching about justification by faith. He did change the emphasis, undoubtedly, in the direction of "faith," what one believes, but that is not a drastic departure from the Old Testament for the "faithfulness" which it expects is surely faithfulness to nothing else but God's truth in which one believes (as Luther said). In the Bible there is no ground for separating faith, what one believes, from faithfulness, how one behaves. Recall how shocked Paul was at the suggestion that since we are justified by faith, saved by grace, it makes no difference then how we behave (Rom. 6). James also had encountered Christians who misunderstood faith and thought it had nothing to do with faithfulness. It was such a misunderstanding, and not Paul's teaching, which he was opposing when he said, "What does it profit, my brethren, if a man says he has faith but has not works? . . . So faith by itself, if it has no works, is dead." (James 2:14, 17) So there is a real continuity between the Old Testament "faithfulness" and the New Testament "faith," even though there was a shift of emphasis in Paul, and in my interpretation of Habakkuk I shall try to show how both are present in his book, even though his emphasis is on faithfulness.

Now let us look at the whole verse in its context and ask ourselves whether we can understand and accept this sentence as an answer to Habakkuk's complaint and as help for us in our times of distress. I have already commented on the difficulty of translating the first half of vs. 4 and must now confess that the immediate context of vs. 4b (i.e. vss. 4a and 5a) is about as difficult as any part of the Old Testament to understand. In the RSV, "but the righteous shall live by his faith," is followed by, "Moreover, wine is treacherous," and somehow that doesn't seem the place for a temperance lesson. This is a really frustrating passage for an exegete, for it seems that now we have come to the pivotal point of the book, and we're not sure what verse 5a means! Again there have been many different suggestions as to how it might be translated, but they fall into three main groups which suggest three rather different meanings, and I shall mention them briefly.

One of the key words in our present Hebrew text is *yayin* "wine" and one group of translations tries to make sense of the line as it stands, e.g.:

> Yea also, because he transgresseth by wine, he is a proud man, neither keepeth at home.   (KING JAMES VERSION)

> But wine cheats the proud man so that he cannot remain.
>   (LUTHER)

Most modern scholars, however, believe the word "wine" may have been the result of a mistake in the copying of early manuscripts and that the original word would have been one which resembles *yayin* but fits the sentence better. There are several words which are possible and these conjectures have produced translations such as:

> As for the traitor in his over-confidence, still less will he ride out the storm, for all his bragging. (NEW ENGLISH BIBLE)

Yet another suggestion has been that the woe-oracles of vss. 6–19 actually began originally with vs. 5, since the word for "wine" looks a little bit like the word for "woe," and this has produced a group of renderings like this:

> Woe to the robber, the insolent tyrant,
>   who is never satisfied! (KARL ELLIGER)

Other modifications of the text have been tried in order to obtain a Hebrew sentence that can be understood, but perhaps we should agree with one able German scholar who admitted he was sure of only one word in the line!

If we find that we cannot have any real confidence (at present) in any of these suggestions, then clearly the crucial question for us is whether there is still a possibility of understanding vs. 4b in terms of its larger context, and I believe that there is. A contrast certainly is being presented between two ways: the way of vs. 4b and that of vs. 4a and possibly also vs. 5a. So "life" in 4b is contrasted with the distortion of the person in 4a, and possibly also with the lack of endurance in 5a. "Righteousness" in 4b is contrasted with that negative quality of which we are uncertain in 4a and perhaps also with treachery and arrogance in 5a. What makes the difference between the two ways is *faithfulness*, and so we must try to see how that speaks to all that has gone before in Habakkuk.

God's answer *leaves* us in that time of waiting to which

2:2–3 refer. The end has not come yet. God has already assured us that the waiting *will* come to an end; that we do not wait in vain. And now he tells us how we can get through that time. In this set of contrasts he has defined the difference between those who believe in him, the righteous, and those who do not. The righteous are they who remain faithful to their God precisely during those times described by Habakkuk in his first chapter, times when faith doesn't make sense. When it does not seem reasonable to believe in a good God, when God's justice and mercy are *not* evident to all, when the righteous do *not* get rewarded for their goodness—precisely then as in no other time do they prove their righteousness by continuing to be faithful.

God's answer puts a good deal on our shoulders—we, with Habakkuk, have come to him for help and he turns it back to us saying, What are *you* going to do now? He gave similar answers to Jeremiah, so I do not think we have misread him here (Jer. 12:5–6, 15:19–21). He calls upon us to hang on and not give up when there is no explainable reason why we shouldn't. But this is a promise, as well. He has not just left us on our own. He assures us that in just such hard times the one who remains faithful shall live. And *life*, as we have come to understand what the Old Testament means by that, is God's best gift. We shall live through it all, we shall not be defeated by the worst that this world can bring. We who have faith in God and are faithful to him will be justified *by the life he gives us.*

This is no intellectual or hypothetical answer. It can only be lived, but it can be lived only if it is believed. It does not yet explain how evil can exist in God's good world. It accepts the fact that evil is here and we suffer from it, but it knows for a certainty that this is, nevertheless, the realm ruled over by the God of justice because of the *experience* of being able to live in a world where evil exists and not be beaten by it. As Raymond Calkins wrote, this verse is a "summons from speculation to action, from questioning to conduct, from brooding to duty."

Examples of the times when faithfulness is needed and of those who have found the faith to live through them are all about us. Once my father was looking through a book on the rural church which I had brought home from seminary and he came across a chapter entitled, "The Difficult Parish." "That fits us," he said, and that became one of the rare occasions in his life when he expressed the frustration he and my mother had experienced in their efforts to serve Christ for some twenty-five years in my home church. They had seen ministers come full of hope and leave discouraged after a few years because of the inability of their fellow church members to understand what the church is all about and to cooperate with those who had some vision. And yet my parents did not quit the church, did not seek another congregation where they might find the fellowship they longed for, did not sow dissension in the parish in order to get their way. They knew that the church needed them, needed all the help it could get. They knew what a negative witness it would be if they— elder, Sunday School superintendent, treasurer, organist—living right next door to the church—began driving to the county seat to worship. And so they continued to be faithful to that congregation until their death without receiving very much of what we all long to get from participation in a Christian fellowship.

They were not alone in that experience. There are many Christians who find their churches to be places which discourage rather than encourage, which are willing to use them but which have little to give in return. And some give it up (let us not be harsh on them!); quit going to worship because they get nothing out of the sermons, quit working because they get criticism instead of thanks, lose all desire to associate with church members whose lives are negative, rather than positive examples of the saving power of Christ. Why should they go on?

But—thank God!—not all do that. Again and again we find Christians who stick it out and keep on giving of themselves, without reward or satisfaction, and through them Christ keeps

the Church alive. Whether or not they know much about Habakkuk, they demonstrate with their lives what he meant by "The
righteous one will live by his faithfulness."

There are other ways. How many marriages have lost their
romance and yet faithfulness endures? I do not mean the mutually
destructive marriages in which each partner is bound to the other
to his and the other's hurt, as in *Who's Afraid of Virginia Woolf?*
I mean the one-sided marriage in which one partner has much to
give but whose own needs are left largely unfulfilled. Once again
that may lead to unfaithfulness, desertion or divorce, but sometimes it does not. Today's society may scorn that person who
chooses to be self-giving instead of using any means to gain one
of our age's highest goals—self-fulfillment. And yet the man or
woman who for some reason chooses to be faithful and to do the
best that is possible for an unrewarding marriage is showing something which the Old Testament calls, in Hebrew, *hesed,* i.e.
steadfast love, covenant love, loyalty to a partner. The Old Testament uses that word of faithfulness in marriage and in other
covenant relationships, and does not scorn it, for it says that is
how God behaves.

I do not know whether our verse may be meaningful to
many who are ill. As one who has never had a chronic illness I
cannot judge, and yet it seems to me that those I have known who
have had little to look forward to in this life except pain and
increasing disability, yet who have not become bitter, have not
given up on life, have relished whatever good they could still find
and have given whatever they had left to give. Surely these people,
whether they ever thought about Habakkuk 2:4 or not, were living
it.

One other example occurs to me: the doubter, the one who
has problems with what to believe and why. Maybe Habakkuk
himself is included here; Job and Ecclesiastes have some claim to
belong. How many people in the church today belong with this
group we can only guess, but we do encounter someone now and

then who will confide his problems to us. And we discover that there are people deeply troubled about what they can honestly believe, people who must be intellectually straight with themselves and cannot accept self-deception. And yet some of them, in spite of their difficulties, do not throw it all over; they are intelligent enough and honest enough to know they have not proved there is no God or disproved the message of the gospel even though there is much they are unsure of. And so they hold on, they continue to be faithful through the dry periods when most of life seems hollow and there is no joy in it. I believe God also justifies the doubter for his faithfulness.

Of course this is not exactly what we want. We would prefer comforting and explanations. And God does not leave us without all comfort and encouragement; it is present in Habakkuk in the promise of life and it is strongly emphasized elsewhere in the Bible, especially in that greatest promise of all, "But I will be with you." (Cf. Exod. 3:12, Judg. 6:16, Jer. 1:8, Isa. 41:10, and cf. Isa. 7:14 with Matt. 1:23). Yet some of his responses to the complaints and pleas of the faithful in the Old Testament put us on the spot, force us to a crisis—we must decide whether we really believe or not. The issue which in Habakkuk has centered on faithfulness is first one of faith; we say we believe God is just and good and in control, but yet the world seems out of control and we come to him asking why? His response is that we live not by sight but by faith. We are not wrong to ask the questions; they are prompted by faith, but the crisis is whether faith can continue without proofs and demonstrations to back it up—i.e. it is a crisis of faithfulness. The demonstrations we ask for belong to the eschaton, the final victory over evil; as long as the end is not yet here, our options are to go on believing in God whether or not we can prove he is Lord of all, or to give it all up.

Habakkuk leaves us in some suspense; he does not immediately tell us which option he has chosen, but chapter 3 of his book will leave no doubt about it. This part of Habakkuk's book has laid before us the first three aspects of what we shall discover to be a remarkably comprehensive account of the relationship between God and the believer who is seriously threatened by evil. The first part is faith, and it underlies all that Habakkuk says in 1:2—2:1. God had revealed himself to the prophet as one who is sovereign and good; Habakkuk believed that with all his heart. The second aspect is produced by the discovery that the world as we experience it does not correspond to what we believe about God as a just sovereign, and so the theodicy problem is born of faith encountering the world. The third aspect is the believer's response to the shock of the reality of evil; will he reject God's truth, or can he be faithful? But this is not the end of God's interaction with us; he does not finally leave it all up to us, as the remainder of this book will make clear. Three more things will happen. There is the continued assurance that evil cannot ultimately prevail—God's word about the future (2:6–19). There is the immediate experience of the presence of God with us, so that we know him not by report but face to face (3:2, 16). And the result of it all is rejoicing, in spite of everything (3:17–18).

CHAPTER III

WOE!

Tyranny is suicide.
          —George Adam Smith

The second section of Habakkuk appears anticlimactic compared with the powerful and moving material which we have just been considering. One interpreter of the book has called it a kind of interlude between the really meaningful materials in chapters one and three. I am not at all sure that is the right judgment to make, but certainly there can be no question that "Woe!" is something of a letdown after "the just shall live by his faith."

Earlier interpreters of the book considered this to be a very important section, however. The prophet had been complaining about the prosperity of the wicked and now finally, in these verses, there appears a clear statement of God's judgment of the evils which Habakkuk protested in chapter one. Calvin, for example, says these verses were added to confirm the teaching that the just live by faith, for he says we could not live by faith unless we were firmly convinced that God cares for us and that the whole world is governed by his providence. He recognized as we do, however, that these words are not God's but those of oppressed peoples, and it is with their character as human words that we shall begin our study.

The section is introduced in vs. 6 as a taunt which will be directed against some unnamed oppressor by the peoples and nations which he had enslaved. Calvin sensed a bit of a problem with making fun of the misfortunes of others, even of the wicked, and I believe we feel the same way and find passages such as this to be among the least attractive to us in the Old Testament, but here is yet another place where modern Biblical research has shed new light so that we can understand better what such texts ought to mean to us.

The Nature of Biblical "Woes"

This second section of Habakkuk is a poem which is clearly divided into five stanzas. Each of the first four begins with "Woe!" and each deals with a different subject, so the basic structure of the poem is easy to determine. When we look carefully at it, however, some peculiarities appear. The fifth stanza begins abruptly and has its "Woe!" in the middle rather than at the beginning. If verses 18 and 19 were interchanged it would look exactly like the others. The first stanza ends with, "for the blood of men and violence to the earth, to cities and all who dwell therein," (vs. 8b) and at the end of the fourth stanza (vs. 17b) we encounter the same words. Is this a refrain, and if so why does it appear only after two stanzas? When we notice that the fourth stanza is longer than the others it may make us wonder whether vs. 17b was really a part of the original composition or whether a scribe copying the book might have added it. These are two fairly clear examples of the way texts could become disrupted when they were copied by hand in antiquity and my translation will reflect the conclusion that Habakkuk's original composition has not been perfectly preserved in the Bible as we now have it. Even with these minor changes the poem remains a bit rough and many other suggestions of possible textual errors have been made by scholars. Later I intend to suggest an alternate explanation for the roughness, however, so will resist the temptation to make any other improvements.

The poem is introduced in vs. 6a as a "taunt" to be sung "in scoffing derision." By whom it is to be sung and against whom it is to be directed the verse does not say, and so we are led back to that difficult verse 5 again. It has spoken of one whose greed is as wide as Sheol, who gathers for himself all nations, i.e. it is an apparent reference to a world-conqueror and his captive peoples. We now begin to see how important vs. 5 is as a transition between the first two units of the book, for we found some reason to connect it with the depiction of the two opposite ways in vs. 4, and now we see that the woes are left without any identification of subject or singer without this verse. When we note that the Chaldean in chapter one has been described as a world-conquering tyrant and that the subject of the woes is depicted in a similar way, then the connection which vs. 5 makes between the two parts becomes clear. God has spoken to the righteous who have been waiting intently for his word, now there is something to be said about the other side. It is not a word from God but human words directed against the tyrant which become another part of God's answer to the righteous.

The word in Hebrew is *hoi,* an exclamation which we have traditionally represented by the English "Woe!" Now in English "Woe to you!" sounds like a threat and in the past the Hebrew word was thought to have the same force and to mean something like "cursed." But modern studies of the word have revealed that it has a range of meanings. It can be a cry of dismay or grief, and when used in that way sometimes our English translations use "alas" instead of "woe" to render it. For example, 1 Kings 13: 11–32 is an account of some of the early prophets in Israel; when one of them was killed by a lion, another buried him in his own tomb, "and they mourned over him, saying, 'Alas, my brother!' " (vs. 30, RSV) Elsewhere we find additional evidence that *hoi* was a cry of grief used by mourners. "Therefore thus says the LORD concerning Jehoiakim the son of Josiah, king of Judah: 'They shall not lament for him, saying, "Ah my brother!" or "Ah sister!" ' " (Jer. 22:18, RSV) ". . . so men shall burn spices for you and lament for you, saying, 'Alas, lord!' " (Jer. 34:5, RSV) "In all the squares there shall be wailing; and in all the streets they shall say, 'Alas! alas!' " (Amos 5:16, RSV)

But mourning sometimes produces emotions other than grief. Sometimes a death arouses anger, because it is untimely or in some other way especially tragic, and if another is at fault in that death the anger may be directed at that person. And we find that the exclamation *hoi* can often be a cry reflecting both sorrow and anger and that it can be addressed to one who is at fault in some way. It has been taken up by the prophets for this purpose. Originally the prophets may have instinctively exclaimed *hoi* when they received from God a message of judgment against their people (like the word Habakkuk received in 1:5–11), reacting in dismay at the message of doom. Then they spoke to their people using the same mournful word, calling them to repentance by mourning over their unhappy future if they did not. "Woe to you who desire the day of the LORD! Why would you have the day of the LORD? It is darkness, and not light." (Amos 5:18)

At other times their tone became more bitter and the cry is followed by a series of accusations, as in Isaiah where two series of woe-speeches may be found (Isa. 5:8–23 continued in 10:1–4, and Isa. 28:1, 29:15, 30:1, 31:1, 33:1) in which the original connection with mourning has virtually disappeared. In Habakkuk we encounter another such series of woes, the tone of which is strikingly bitter and harsh, but I shall attempt to show later that the memory of the funereal setting of the word is still present and that the passage is actually a parody of a funeral song.

But first a new translation must be attempted. The translations we normally use put their primary emphasis on accuracy in rendering the meaning of the Hebrew words and syntax into English, and that is as it should be. But in a passage such as this a good deal is lost in such translations. For this is parody, the language is almost slangy in its sarcasm and its use of alliteration; but in our English versions it tends to come out solemn and proper. So I shall try to offer an alternate translation which strives at capturing the feeling of the Hebrew language and which is thus very free in its approach to the text. It should never be taken in place of the translations which strive for accuracy but perhaps ought to be read along with them to supply what they have lost. This is not a great work of poetic art; the stanzas are not all the same length and the lines are irregular. The third stanza seems to get off the subject somewhat, as compared with the others. Yet I do not propose to try to recover a more perfect, hypothetical original, as others have done. The poem reminds me of other popular ditties, ancient and modern, in these respects, and I suspect that Habakkuk has taken up the flavor of derisive popular songs of his day at this point in his work because that expresses very well what needs to be said.

Somehow "woe" does not seem to be the best English word to use in a translation such as I propose; it sounds a bit stodgy. Others have tried "alas," but that may also be too formal. I would like to try "Oh!" as a word which, though not as strong as *hoi*, can convey many overtones of meaning. Like *hoi* it can be an expression of distress, as in "Oh no!" or of mockery, as in "Oh ho!" So we shall read the poem in this way:

Will not all of them take up a parody against   (6)
    him and a derisive riddle about him,
        saying:
Oh, you multiplier of that which is not yours!
    How long? Collector of unpaid debts!
Will not your creditors suddenly arise,   (7)
    and men awake who will make you tremble
    so that you will become their plunder?
Since you have pillaged many nations,   (8)
    what's left of the peoples will pillage you,
    because of murder, violence done to the land,
    the city, and everyone who dwells in it.

Oh, you profiteer, building your estate on evil,   (9)
    setting your nest up high,
    insuring it from misfortune.
You have devised shame for your house,   (10)
    cutting off many people,
    —and losing your own life.
For the stone will cry out from the wall,   (11)
    and the plaster to the woodwork respond.

Oh, you builder of a city—with blood,   (12)
    and founder of a city on iniquity,
(Is it not indeed from Yahweh of Hosts?)   (13)
That people toil only enough for fire,
    and populations are weary for nothing.
For the earth shall be filled with the knowledge   (14)
    of the glory of Yahweh,
      as the waters cover the sea.

Oh, you giver of drink to your neighbor
    (joining your wrath)   (15)
    until he is drunk,
      so that you may gaze on their nakedness.
You shall be satiated with dishonor instead
    of glory.   (16)
Drink! You also, and show your uncircumcision!
The cup of Yahweh's right hand will come round to you
    and dishonor will cover your glory.
For the violence of Lebanon shall cover you,   (17)
    and the destruction of beasts will terrorize
    you.

Oh, you invoker of wood, with "Awake!"   (19)
    with, "Arouse yourself!" to the dumb stone.
      Can it teach?
Look, it is sheathed with gold and silver,
    but there is no spirit inside it!
What benefit is to be got from an image   (18)
    whose maker has imagined it—
    a cast statue, a teacher of lies!
For the artisan trusts in his own art
    when he makes stolid statues.
But Yahweh is in his holy temple.   (20)
Hush before him, all the earth!

As we consider now what this section contributes to the
book and whether it is integrally related with what precedes and

follows three questions may guide our thinking: To whom does it apply? What does it mean, as a unit following 1:2—2:4? What good does it do us, really?

To Whom Does It Apply?

This is another of the much-debated questions in the history of the study of Habakkuk. Long ago the people of the Qumran Community who produced their own Habakkuk Commentary identified the tyrant with their own enemies. For others the main debate has been whether the tyrant is the prophet's own king, a Judean ruler such as Jehoiakim (2 Kings 24:1–9, Jer. 22:18–23), or whether he is a foreign king, either of the Assyrians or the Babylonians. The reason that the debate is possible is that there are no definite historical references in the section at all. What is described there has occurred over and over again, and not only in antiquity. The prophet speaks of those who wrongfully enrich themselves, who have plundered many nations, of those who live in luxury and security at the expense of the poor, of those who make use of liquor to shame their neighbors, and of worshippers of idols. It is my conclusion that no effort has been made in this song to refer to any specific situation in history; rather that it has purposely been expressed in general terms which could apply again and again to tyranny in many forms. My belief that this is intentional is supported by the general nature of the language in the first section of the book. We saw there how Habakkuk used the traditional language of worship, words which must be applicable to more than one situation in order to be useful to the worshipping community, instead of producing his own complaint dealing with a specific situation. I believe that Habakkuk used both kinds of material, liturgical language in chapter one, and echoes of popular songs in chapter two, because he had already recognized that the issue which concerned him went far beyond the problems of Judah early in the sixth century, catastrophic though they were. I believe that Habakkuk had learned something from the wisdom teachers of Israel whose vision had already reached beyond the confines of Israel itself in order to deal with those aspects of human existence which we all have in common. My own studies of Habakkuk have shown how closely his book is related to the wisdom literature of the Old Testament and especially to that part of wisdom which takes up the problems of suffering and of God's justice (Job, Ecclesiastes). But long before I did my work, George Adam Smith found in Habakkuk 2 something that reminded him of Hebrew Wisdom, what he called "the attempt to uncover the moral processes of life and express a philosophy of history." And he went on to say, "These *proverbs* or *taunt-songs*, in conformity with the proverbs of later Wisdom, dwell upon the inherent tendency to decay of all injustice. Tyranny, they assert, and history has confirmed them—tyranny is suicide." We have not been successful in identifying the particular tyrant against whom Habakkuk was speaking, then, because the prophet's concerns were broader than that. He had already begun to develop a universal outlook and so he used language which could apply to tyranny whenever and wherever it arises.

These subjects of which Habakkuk sings—are they not depressingly familiar to us? Those who get rich because of other men's debts; those whose wealth goes into immense and luxurious homes for themselves, complete with the latest security devices; those who build cities on the blood of the poor; those who profit by and ruin their fellow men through strong drink—was Habakkuk writing in the seventh century or the twentieth? To whom does it apply? We answer, if the shoe fits.

What Does It Mean, As a Unit Following 1:2—2:4?

Is there a relationship between the first and second sections of Habakkuk? I suggested at the end of chapter two that the whole book is a unity and that it takes us through six stages of the believer's life with God, but now it is up to me to show that the

connection really does exist. After all, prophetic books are an-
thologies of works produced at various times and for different
purposes, and it could be that the second section did not have the
same concerns as the first. So I shall be trying to show, in this
chapter and the next, that the book is a little like a liturgy, using
various types of literature, it is true, but putting them together
in such a way as to form a thematic whole.

We have learned that "Woe!" was in Israel originally a cry
of mourning, and I have followed up that clue to reach the
conclusion that Habakkuk 2:6–19 is a parody of a Hebrew funeral
song or dirge. Since the truth of that statement is not immediately
evident to the modern reader some justification for it should be
offered.

Burial, in the Middle East, normally took place on the same
day as death, and was done in the family tomb which usually was
a chamber cut into the rock. The "professionals" at the funeral
were the singers, members of the community, apparently usually
women, who were skilled at singing appropriate songs of mourning. (We have more professionals at our funerals, but they still
often include the singer and musician and a traditional body of
appropriate music.) These women are referred to by Jeremiah:

> Thus says the LORD of hosts:
>> "Consider, and call for the mourning women to come;
>> send for the skilful women to come;
> let them make haste and raise a wailing over us,
>> that our eyes may run down with tears,
>> and our eyelids gush with water."   (JER. 9:17–18)

> Hear, O women, the word of the LORD,
>> and let your ear receive the word of his mouth,
> teach to your daughters a lament,
>> and each to her neighbor a dirge.
> For death has come up into our windows,
>> it has entered our palaces,
> cutting off the children from the streets

and the young men from the squares.

(JER. 9:20–21)

The songs they sang were for the most part traditional, but it seems likely that they re-composed them to fit each occasion; such is the nature of oral tradition. We have one good example of such a dirge in the Old Testament, the song which David sang at the death of Saul and Jonathan (2 Sam. 1:19–27). We should note certain features of that song which seem to be typical of dirges: the emphasis on the greatness of the deceased as a way of expressing the enormity of one's loss ("From the blood of the slain, from the fat of the mighty, the bow of Jonathan turned not back, and the sword of Saul returned not empty. Saul and Jonathan, beloved and lovely! In life and in death they were not divided; they were swifter than eagles, they were stronger than lions"); the concern that this death might be a cause for rejoicing among the deceased's enemies ("Tell it not in Gath, publish it not in the streets of Ashkelon; lest the daughters of the Philistines rejoice, lest the daughters of the uncircumcised exult"); and the theme of reversal of fortune ("How are the mighty fallen!"). Each of these motifs appears with a new use in Habakkuk 2. But there is a tradition of the prophetic use of funeral songs which lies between the true dirge of 2 Samuel 1 and the woe-song of Habakkuk. Sometimes the prophets created their own dirges for a new purpose, to express grief at the impending death of the nation Israel, as Amos did when he sang, "Fallen, no more to rise, is the virgin Israel; forsaken on her land, with none to raise her up." (Amos 5:2) Or they used them as part of their description of how God would judge the great nations of the earth, as Ezekiel did when he said that at the fall of the city Tyre all the princes of the sea would go into mourning and would sing:

> How you have vanished from the seas,
>   O city renowned,
> that was mighty on the sea,

you and your inhabitants,
who imposed your terror
on all the mainland!
Now the isles tremble
on the day of your fall;
Yea, the isles that are in the sea
are dismayed at your passing. (EZEK. 26:17–18)

The emphasis is still on the greatness of the one that is gone and
on reversal of fortune, and the tone is still one of grief, but in
other prophetic uses of the dirge the tone is changed completely
and they have produced what can only be called a parody of the
funeral song. The masterpiece of this type is to be found in Isaiah
14:4–21, which is a song to be sung at the death of some unnamed
king of Babylon, a great tyrant, and it is to be sung by those whom
he had enslaved to express their joy that at last he is dead. They
do so by singing a mock funeral song, using the theme of reversal
of fortune as a cause for glee rather than mourning, emphasizing
the former power and prestige of the man as a way of gloating over
his present weakness.

How the oppressor has ceased,
the insolent fury ceased!
. . . .
Your pomp is brought down to Sheol,
the sound of your harps;
maggots are the bed beneath you,
and worms are your covering.
. . . .
Is this the man who made the earth tremble,
who shook kingdoms?
. . . .
All the kings of the nations lie in glory,
each in his own tomb;
but you are cast out, away from your sepulchre. . . .
(ISA. 14:4, 11, 16, 18F.)

The rhythm and typical language of the dirge are still used extensively by Isaiah; when we turn back to the song in Habakkuk we have moved a step away from the formal pattern of the funeral song, but there are still enough similarities that we should also interpret this passage as a mock dirge. The old mourning cry "Woe!" is regularly used; the death of the subject is described (vs. 10); his dishonor is emphasized (vss. 7–8, 16–17; cf. Isa. 14:10–11, 18–20); the rejoicing of his enemies which in a true dirge would be a cause for grief now is to be felt in the malicious glee of the singer; the greatness of the subject's former power is described (vss. 8, 9, 12; cf. Isa. 14:6, 16–17); and the reversal of fortune (vss. 7, 8, 10, 16, 17) is now the occasion for celebration. One additional point of comparison between Habakkuk 2 and Isaiah 14 is that both are introduced by a Hebrew word, *mashal.* This word is usually translated "proverb," but here that is clearly not exactly what the word means. In these two passages (and also in Micah 2:4) it seems to indicate that one type of literature, the dirge, is being used for a new purpose, as a taunt song, and so maybe it ought to be translated by a word such as "parody."

Habakkuk announces that the nations and peoples will sing a mock funeral song when this tyrant dies. Unfortunately the song he records is a little premature. The tyrant isn't yet dead. The prophet and his people still squirm under the thumb of his repressive rule. We know that Habakkuk will never live to see things any better. But God has authorized them to celebrate the tyrant's death ahead of time, and that was his way of reasserting that it is He, and no one else, who rules the world.

The tyrant has reversed God's order. That is what the prophet has been complaining about. "The wicked surround the righteous, so justice goes forth perverted. . . . The wicked swallows up the man more righteous than he." And why, he has asked, does God do nothing about it? God now declares that the attempted and apparently successful reversal of his order is about to rebound against the tyrant one day. He cannot reverse God's order forever and with impunity.

He is going to die some day. And death ought to be an occasion for mourning. It's only the normal thing to mourn at someone's death; that's only human. But not at this man's death. His funeral will become a holiday and those who might have been his mourners will sing no dirges but will instead make parodies of funeral songs as they celebrate. There will be something very wrong with that funeral, and the prophet tells us this is God's way of demonstrating that there was something very wrong with that man's life.

The taunt songs which oppressed peoples sing when their overlords die are one of God's brusque ways of telling us that he does *not* overlook the wickedness of those who oppress his faithful people, for in his own time, at the right time, judgment does come.

But, What Good Does That Do Us, Really?

Perhaps we may be forgiven for thinking that's little enough comfort. What real good does it do to tell a suffering people, "Just be patient, the old boy's bound to die someday"? Tyrants outlive too many of their victims. I expect Habakkuk knew that, too, and that partly accounts for what he says in chapter three, for there he speaks in very personal terms of what it means to him to go on living even though God has not yet straightened everything out for us.

Yet in this chapter he has recorded these taunt songs as something apparently meaningful to him. Elsewhere in the Old Testament other authors have addressed themselves to the powerful men of their day, as well—to rebuke, to threaten judgment— and in studying those passages I have been faced by the same question: "What were they trying to accomplish?" When Isaiah spoke to the king of Assyria:

> Because you have raged against me
> and your arrogance has come to my ears,
> I will put my hook in your nose

and my bit in your mouth,
and I will turn you back on the way
by which you came,   (ISA. 37:29)

did he think Sennacherib would hear those words somehow and
be swayed by them? He wasn't. Is there any likelihood that the
many foreign kings addressed by the prophets (e.g. Jer. 46–51,
Ezek. 25–32) even heard any of those messages, let alone believed
them? If not, what is their point?

I believe there is something positive that can be said about
the value of such texts and I base it on remarks made by George
Adam Smith, in his commentary on Isaiah, about the Atheism of
Force and the Atheism of Fear.

When a nation or ruler achieves power enough to determine
the destiny of the rest of the world, as Assyria and Babylonia did
in antiquity and as the United States and Russia have done in our
lifetimes, then it becomes a very great danger that a virtual deifi-
cation of the power to govern will occur. That has been obvious
enough to us in dictatorships such as Hitler's where all the trap-
pings of religion were made to support the rule of one man, but
it has only been recently that we have begun to recognize that the
same thing has been occurring in a more insidious way in our own
country. The power to rule becomes the sole aim of the ruler's
activity and the sole guide for deciding what is right and wrong.
God, if he needs to be considered at all, is on the side with the
strongest battalions. The ruler uses God for his own purposes by
manipulating his servants. That is the Atheism of Force. Power
is deified when those who have it refuse to accept any moral
controls on how they use it. The Assyrian kings used to boast of
that publicly in their royal inscriptions; only recently have we
learned of the private ruminations of our own leaders on that
subject.

Power is also deified when those *against whom* it is wielded
panic in the face of it and agree that there is no other kind of

strength that matters. That is the Atheism of Fear. It appears in many forms among us. When we complain that government has become so big and so corrupt that there is really nothing we can do about it, when we are tempted to give up scruples about the proper use of power and to adopt the methods of the powerful and unscrupulous because only they seem to succeed—then we have fallen a victim to the Atheism of Fear.

Now the tyrant may never hear Habakkuk's message, or if he does hear it may only laugh—his own might is his god! The message ought to be addressed to the tyrant anyway, for who knows whether he may hear after all and whether there may be a chance that he will change. But we know from history that the likelihood of that is small. There are few converts from the Atheism of Force. However, when the oppressed hear it, when the weak who cannot stand up to the power of their ruler and those who suffer and cannot fight back are assured that there is a power greater than the tyrant—if they believe it (the just shall live by his faith) then they have God's word for it that there are other kinds of power, God's word for it that against all appearances he is still in control, and they can be freed from the Atheism of Fear. "The body they may kill; God's truth abideth still."

Or is that wishful thinking? That body, after all, which goes hungry and suffers and which they sometimes kill with impunity, is pretty important. And if only 23% of the crimes reported in this country in the 70s are being solved, there is a lot of evil being gotten away with, not to mention the suffering inflicted on our fellow men which is not even classified as crime. And in our darker moments it may be very hard not to admit that the wicked really are stronger than the forces of righteousness and that God, if he is involved at all, is rather too far removed from the scene of action to be of any significant help. When we read in the Bible that God punishes the wicked and rewards the righteous in very direct ways, it tends to rub against the grain of our "realism," for we immediately begin to tally all the exceptions we can think of, and by doing so are giving way to the Atheism of Fear, for the exceptions begin to dominate our thinking.

Does history confirm those dark thoughts? If the wicked really are stronger than the forces of righteousness, as *they* think, and if the wicked really go unpunished more often than not, as *we* think in our gloomier moments, then how is it that wickedness has not won the day long before now? Why does not the completely unscrupulous use of power wipe out the scrupulous, if that kind of power and that lack of moral restraint is really so unbeatable as the Atheism of Force and the Atheism of Fear tell us? Why haven't the forces of evil smashed all resistance long ago? Why are there any righteous left? The answer must be that there really is something else going on in this world. There really is a force —and we know who it is: it is Yahweh, the God and Father of our Lord Jesus Christ—greater than armies, bombs, bribery, and torture, and it is he who thwarts the efforts of the wicked and gives to the righteous another kind of power (not of this world, the New Testament says) to enable them to resist and to endure.

Examples of this truth could be multiplied from the histories of the people who have lived by the Bible, Jews and Christians, but let me give only one which is close to us now, the experiences of blacks in America. Slavery attempted to impress the Atheism of Fear upon them, and indeed we see its partial success in the servile attitude which blacks had to adopt for many years in order to survive in our culture. But the gospel was always among them as a subversive element telling them that the Atheism of Fear was a lie, and many have agreed that this was the one thing they had that kept them from giving in completely. A modern black preacher, I. T. Bradley, has put it this way:

> You are going to human communities,
>   and you're calling it urban renewal,
> and you are land-grabbing,
>   putting folk out of homes.

You create a condition and you put a man on welfare,
  and then you tell him he is there because he is lazy.
Then you closed up your schools
  and wouldn't let him go in there.
And then you moved out into the suburbs
  and you wouldn't let him cross that track.

  And he kept on saying,
"There is a brighter day coming by and by."
Every now and then he would go down in his heart
and he would say,
  "Up above my head I hear music in the air,
    there must be a God somewhere."
You told him he was nobody
  But he kept on saying,
  "I'm a child of the King,
    I am a child of the King,
  Jesus is my savior,
    And I am a child of the King."
You got your police force together,
  and you made your security in your army,
  and you made your security in your national guard.
  And we kept on singing,
"He's got the whole world in his hand,
  and he's got the little bitty baby in his hand,
And he's got me and you, brother, in his hand."
  ("God's Redeeming Love," *Perspective* 13 [1972], p. 124.)

That serenity in the midst of turmoil which those gospel
songs convey is an echo of what now happens in Habakkuk, for
after the turbulence of fighting against this life's injustices, after
the bitterness of the condemnation of those who oppress us, he
startles us with a completely new voice, with the quietness and
serenity of his next to last word:

Yahweh is in his holy temple.
All the earth—Hush before him!

CHAPTER IV

YET I WILL REJOICE!

And when every blessing's flown,
Love Thee for Thyself alone.
            —A. L. BARBAULD

As we begin the third chapter of Habakkuk we encounter
a new title, "A Prayer of Habakkuk the prophet according to
Shigionoth." This raises some questions about whether we are
beginning something really new at this point. Is chapter three
really connected with the preceding chapters so that they are to
be read together as having some continuity, or is this a separate
piece with no relationship to the rest and only included here
because it was also ascribed to Habakkuk? If there is continuity,
why the separate title? These are problems which have puzzled
scholars for years and many of them have concluded that this
chapter does not really belong with the rest. When the Habakkuk
Commentary was discovered at Qumran a few years ago and it
was found that only chapters one and two were included in that
work, that seemed to a good many to settle the matter; chapter
three was not a part of the original book. But I think the question
is not to be solved quite so simply as that. As others have pointed
out, it may well have been that the commentator did not find that
the last chapter fit his interests, so that he used only the parts of
the book which served his purposes well. My conclusion is that
whether or not the three chapters were produced originally as a
whole piece, at present they are unified thematically, and I believe
that is not accidental but the intentional work of either Habakkuk
himself or an editor of his work. The nature of that thematic unity
will be explored as we get into the chapter.

A Psalm of Habakkuk

Chapter three not only possesses a title but also has at the
beginning and end notations which presumably are instructions

for its performance. Such notations, which are well known to us from the Psalter, have been notoriously difficult to translate since they are full of technical terms which do not occur elsewhere in the Bible. The RSV does not try to translate Shigionoth at all, taking it as probably the name of the tune to which the psalm was to be sung. The last line of the chapter is translated "To the choirmaster: with stringed instruments." So, just as we found internal clues in the first chapter which revealed a relationship between Habakkuk and the Psalms, here we find technical notations at the beginning and end of the poem which point in the same direction. Compare the note at the beginning of Psalm 4, as just one example. These rubrics can scarcely mean anything other than that the poems to which they refer were sung in public performance.

Now we must ask a question prompted by that problem of the unity of the book which has already been raised. When was this song first sung? Was it a standard part of the repertoire for the temple singers of the seventh century B.C. which at some time or other was included with the sayings of Habakkuk because his name was attached to both? Or were the technical notes added to one chapter of Habakkuk's book because this particular part of his work was excerpted at some time for use in worship?

A form critical analysis of the poem strongly supports the former suggestion, since its form is comparable to several psalms of lament and of thanksgiving. It is different in its emphasis from the laments with which we were comparing chapter one in that, unlike them, it does not concentrate on the psalmists' complaints. This kind concentrates instead on the description of how God comes to help those who call upon him in need. So we find in this chapter only a few references to the trials of the psalmist and his people, but an extensive description of how God comes, in his great power, to save them, and also expressions of the psalmist's certainty that God is his savior. These elements occur typically in both laments and thanksgivings in the Psalter. In the laments God's mighty deeds are recounted for several purposes: to encourage the sufferer, perhaps as reminders to God himself at times, and sometimes as ways of expressing the psalmist's puzzlement that God has not yet intervened to help him (cf. e.g. Pss. 11, 31, 77). In the thanksgivings they form a natural part of the worshipper's expressions of praise to God for his gracious power which has redeemed him (cf. Pss. 9, 18, 30, 111). So in form, content, and its instructions for performance, Habakkuk 3 is clearly a song intended to be sung in worship.

If the chapter is still to be connected with chapters 1—2, as I have suggested it should be, then two options seem possible in the light of what we have discovered about its essential nature. (a) Some modern scholars have suggested that the whole book was written to be used in worship, that the whole thing is a liturgy containing complaints, oracles, woes, and concluding with a psalm of thanksgiving. The many clues which we have found connecting Habakkuk with worship in the Jerusalem temple tend to support such an idea; however, we do not know anything about a worship service which would include all these elements and so the suggestion must remain a hypothesis. (b) It might also be that only chapter three was written for worship, but that its message was so appropriate an expression of Habakkuk's faith as a result of the experiences recalled for us in the first two chapters, that at some time it was added to those chapters as an authentic expression of the way this prophet resolved his theological problem. That the combination of the three chapters was for the intention of producing a thematic whole is further suggested by the occurrence elsewhere of similar patterns. In the book of Job, the dialogue, full of complaints and discussions of the justice of God, is eventually followed by a theophany, the appearance of God himself. The pattern in Habakkuk is the same, since the most prominent element in chapter three is, as we shall soon see, a theophany. Similar patterns occur in thanksgivings and psalms of lament in the Psalter; all of which suggests that it is correct to interpret the whole book as a unit. So I find in this chapter two more stages in the believer's experience of God which are necessary complements of the four which have appeared earlier.

When we look at the subject matter of the psalm three important features appear which require our attention before we can understand fully what the poem means: theophany, myth, and history.

Theophany. This term is used to denote the appearances of God in the Old Testament which are described in a very physical way. The classic example is the way the presence of God on Mount Sinai is represented. "And the LORD said to Moses, 'Lo, I am coming to you in a thick cloud.' " (Exod. 19:9) "On the morning of the third day there were thunders and lightnings, and a thick cloud upon the mountain, and a very loud trumpet blast, so that all the people who were in the camp trembled." (Exod. 19:16) "And Mount Sinai was wrapped in smoke, because the LORD descended upon it in fire; and the smoke went up like the smoke of a kiln, and the whole mountain quaked greatly. And as the sound of the trumpet grew louder and louder, Moses spoke, and God answered him in thunder." (Exod. 19:18f) Elsewhere in the Bible the coming of God is described with similar imagery, but the examples which will interest us most are those which occur in poems of the same type as Habakkuk 3, viz. the psalms of lament and of thanksgiving. Psalm 18 is a very helpful one; it begins with words of praise to God his deliverer and then moves to a brief reference to the distress from which he had asked to be saved (vss. 1–3, 4–6a). The response from God was in the form of theophany:

> Then the earth reeled and rocked;
>> the foundations also of the mountains trembled
>> and quaked, because he was angry.
> Smoke went up from his nostrils,
>> and devouring fire from his mouth;
>> glowing coals flamed forth from him.
> He bowed the heavens, and came down;

thick darkness was under his feet.
He rode on a cherub, and flew;
   he came swiftly upon the wings of the wind.
He made darkness his covering around him,
   his canopy thick clouds dark with water.
Out of the brightness before him
   there broke through his clouds
   hailstones and coals of fire.
The LORD also thundered in the heavens,
   and the Most High uttered his voice,
   hailstones and coals of fire.
And he sent out his arrows, and scattered them;
   he flashed forth lightnings, and routed them.
Then the channels of the sea were seen,
   and the foundations of the world were laid bare,
at thy rebuke, O LORD,
   at the blast of the breath of thy nostrils.

Then the psalmist goes on to describe his rescue and to praise God at length for his salvation. What is important to us is that elements which appeared in the Sinai theophany: earthquake, smoke, fire, thick clouds, and the voice of God like thunder, are combined with a warlike tone (especially in vss. 14f, but vs. 7 also refers to the anger of God) and references to the sea (vs. 15 and also 16: "He reached from on high, he took me, he drew me out of many waters"); for the depiction of God as a warrior who is victorious over the waters is even more prominent in Habakkuk 3. That this combination of terrifying natural phenomena along with the depiction of God as a warrior was one of the traditional ways of speaking of God in ancient Israel is proven by the occurrence of the same elements in numerous other places. We shall stick to the Psalms for our examples.

Our God comes, he does not keep silence,
   before him is a devouring fire,
   round about him a mighty tempest.
                                  (PS. 50:3)

O God, when thou didst go forth before thy people,
 when thou didst march through the wilderness,
the earth quaked, the heavens poured down rain,
 at the presence of God;
yon Sinai quaked at the presence of God,
 the God of Israel.   (PS. 68:7F.)
Sing to God, O kingdoms of the earth;
 sing praises to the Lord,
to him who rides in the heavens, the ancient heavens;
 lo, he sends forth his voice, his mighty voice.
            (PS. 68:32F.)

Psalm 77 is a lament containing a more lengthy description of the psalmist's troubles leading to his meditation on the mighty deeds of God in the past in this form:

When the waters saw thee, O God,
 when the waters saw thee, they were afraid,
 yea the deep trembled.
The clouds poured out water;
 the skies gave forth thunder;
 thy arrows flashed on every side.
The crash of thy thunder was in the whirlwind;
 thy lightnings lighted up the world;
 the earth trembled and shook.
Thy way was through the sea,
 thy path through the great waters;
 yet thy footprints were unseen.
Thou didst lead thy people like a flock
 by the hand of Moses and Aaron.   (PS. 77:16–20)

Most of this imagery seems to have originated in the distant past from the association of the coming of God himself with the occurrence of violent storms and perhaps volcanic activity and earthquakes. Some think that the Sinai experience must have occurred at an active volcano in order to account for the phenomena described in Exodus 19; others believe the imagery is essentially based on the storm. Neither origin provides a very good explanation for the victory over the waters which also appears in theophanies, so it seems most likely that we are faced by a composite of images drawn from the most awesome elements in the natural world, used freely and poetically in an effort to represent the emotional effect of experiencing the immediate presence of God himself. I shall have some additional suggestions to make about what was really happening when the Israelites said they had experienced a theophany in a later section.

Myth. There are two sets of mythological texts known to us now which bear some remarkable resemblances to parts of Habakkuk 3. One is the well-known Babylonian creation epic, *Enuma Elish*, in which Marduk is depicted as a mighty warrior using various elements of nature as weapons in order to defeat Tiamat, who represents the watery chaos. The other is the Baal epic found at Ugarit (modern Ras Shamra), in which Baal is called the "rider on the clouds," is obviously associated with the thunderstorm, and is in conflict with Yam, the sea. These resemblances have led some scholars to say that Habakkuk 3 is patterned on one or the other text, but I think there is a more likely explanation.

Despite the differences in culture between Egypt and Canaan, Canaan and Mesopotamia, there was still a great deal of interchange of ideas, symbols, and even religious and literary themes amongst the peoples of the ancient Near East. The more we learn of those other cultures the clearer it becomes that Israel did not live in isolation but was exposed to and shared in the common heritage of the entire ancient world. We know that heritage included a widespread recognition of the *storm god,* called by different names (e.g. Baal, Hadad) but described in much the same way everywhere. Furthermore, the theme of combat between a deity and the Waters (of chaos—Tiamat, of the sea—Yam) is a common one which is developed in a variety of forms. Among the elements of the natural world which tended to be deified were such disasters as plague and pestilence. (Resheph, the Hebrew word translated "pestilence" in vs. 5, is well-known as a minor deity.)

Habakkuk 3 clearly contains echoes of these elements from the myths of the ancient Near East. Yahweh is described the way the storm god was represented in other religions (vss. 3–4, 10–11). His triumph over the waters, involving as it does anger and conflict (vss. 8–9, 15) goes beyond the memory of the crossing of the Red Sea, which no doubt is present here, to refer to a kind of hostility between God and nature which is common in myth but unusual for the Yahwistic creation faith. And there is a kind of personification: of plague and pestilence (vs. 5), of the rivers, sea and mighty waters (vss. 8, 10, 15), and of God's chariot with its name "Salvation" (vs. 8), which is also to be found in mythological texts. So the relationships seem undeniable.

But this is not to say that Habakkuk 3 is a mythical text or even that it is a Yahwistic re-writing of some specific work such as *Enuma Elish*. It is poetry, and poetry in the Old Testament as elsewhere is both more conservative and more daring than prose; more conservative in that it preserves archaic language and symbols which have ceased to be used in prose, and more daring in that it will "play with" imagery which carries dangerous connotations, overtones which reasoned discourse would have to deny. So we find more obvious echoes of ancient Near Eastern myth in Old Testament poetry than in prose, for vivid poetic language is easily remembered and tends to be retained unchanged for a long time—even beyond the time when the ideas it conveys have been challenged. The imagery which we encounter in Habakkuk 3 had evidently remained a part of the Israelite's "culture," his knowledge of the world around him, and even though it might not fully agree with the rational understanding of Yahweh which someone like Habakkuk perhaps could have written in prose, it continued to be used in the language of *worship* which, as we well know, tends to preserve archaisms longer than almost any other body of literature. As I hope to show later, it was also probably more appropriate language than prose could possibly provide for the expression of those religious experiences which are presumed to lie behind it.

History. Modern Old Testament studies have emphasized the central importance of history to Israel. When an Israelite confessed his faith, spoke of his God, he told what God had done for his chosen people (cf. Deut. 26, Joshua 24, Neh. 9, Pss. 78, 105—107). That way of speaking about God dominates most of the Old Testament, with certain notable exceptions, mainly the Wisdom Literature: Proverbs, Ecclesiastes, and Job. It has been mentioned earlier that Habakkuk shows a close relationship to Israelite Wisdom, and in chapters 1 and 2, where the influence of Wisdom is prominent, there are no references to Israel's history.

Chapter 3 is a bit more traditional, perhaps, in that we are reminded of God's mighty acts in the past by a series of key words. There is nothing like a recital, but to one who knew the sacred history the words would have been enough to recall how God had intervened on behalf of his people in the past. I have already noted that although nothing explicit is said about the Exodus, words such as "You trampled the sea with your horses, the foam of mighty waters (vs. 15, cf. vss. 8, 9)" could not have failed to remind the Israelite of that archetypal saving event. Compare the song of Miriam: "Sing to the LORD, for he has triumphed gloriously; the horse and his rider he has thrown into the sea (Exod. 15:21)," and the part of Psalm 77 quoted earlier. Our assumption that any statement about victory over the waters would recall to the Israelite first and foremost the Exodus is supported by the other historical allusions in this chapter, all of which refer to the period of wandering in the wilderness and early settlement in Canaan.

In vs. 3 God is said to come from Teman and Mount Paran, places to the south of Palestine in the region of Edom. These are presumably references to a route which might be taken from Sinai to the promised land, since Sinai and Paran are paralleled as designations of the place from which God comes to save in Deuteronomy 33:2. The words should be taken, then, as allusions to both the Sinai and Wilderness traditions (Num. 10:12, 12:16, 13:3, 26) in the early history of Israel. "Cushan," in vs. 7, is a word which appears nowhere else in the Bible, but since it appears here in parallel with Midian it seems likely that it is a poetic shortening of Cushanrishathaim, one of the oppressors of the Israelites during the period of the Judges (Judges 3:8–10). Trouble with Midian is recorded in passages which bracket this reference, in the Wilderness materials of Numbers 25 and 31 and in the Gideon story (Judges 6—8).

Each of these brief allusions, then, may be understood as signals to the Israelite which would recall to him times in his early history when God came from his ancient dwelling place (not Jerusalem, take note) in order to deliver his people from their enemies by waging holy war against them. The historical references are so brief that we would not be justified in spending a great deal of time here on the meaning of history for Israel's faith, yet the fact that they occur at all has its significance and we shall find it necessary when we begin to put all the elements of this psalm together to consider a bit further the value of history for faith.

But first we must listen to the song.

A Problem in Translation

The possibility of archaisms and the presence of somewhat extravagant poetic language in the chapter have already been mentioned, but now they arise to taunt the would-be translator. Frankly, there is universal uncertainty about what, exactly, some of the lines of this poem mean. Conjectures and suggested emendations abound, but this author feels perhaps unduly reticent to accept very many of the suggestions as being even likely, let alone really convincing. Unfortunately, without conjecture some lines

simply cannot be translated, and I have finally decided that it
might be well for the reader to know what uncertainty scholars
experience with certain brief portions of the Old Testament text,
so I have left some lines, where a great deal of guesswork is
involved, untranslated. Unsatisfactory though that may be for all
of us, perhaps it is better to admit that we do not know than to
pretend that we do. It is to be hoped that the resulting omissions
will not unduly harm the powerful effect which the poem should
have on the reader.

> Yahweh, I have heard your story; (2)
> > I am awed, Yahweh, by your work.
> In the midst of years, revive it;
> > In the midst of years, make it known;
> Amid turmoil remember mercy.
>
> The Deity is coming from Teman (3)
> > and the Holy One from Mount Paran.
> His splendor covered the heavens
> > and the earth was full of his praise.
> He has the brilliance of light, (4)
> > rays from his hand,
> > and there his power is hidden.
> Ahead of him goes plague (5)
> > and pestilence follows his steps.
> He stood and measured Earth: (6)
> > he looked and the nations lept up,
> And the ancient mountains were shattered,
> > the enduring hills bowed down,
> > the enduring ways are his.
> > (. . . . .) (7)
> The tents of Cushan are in turmoil,
> > the curtains of the land of Midian.
> Was it with the rivers you were angry, Yahweh? (8)
> > with the rivers your wrath,
> > or with the Sea your fury?
> That you rode on your horses,

your chariot 'Salvation'?
You stripped your bow clean
 (. . . . .)   (9)
 you cleft Earth with rivers.
The mountain saw you and writhed,   (10)
 torrents of water swept over,
The Deep uttered its voice,
 it lifted its hands on high.
Sun, Moon stood in their realm;   (11)
 for light your arrows went forth,
 for brightness the flash of your spear.
With rage you strode the earth,   (12)
 with anger you sought the nations.
You went out for the salvation of your people,   (13)
 for the salvation of your anointed.
You crushed the head of the house of the wicked,
 laying bare the base of his neck;
You pierced with his shaft the head (. . .)   (14)
(. . . . .)
(. . . . .)
You trampled the Sea with your horses,   (15)
 the foam of Mighty Waters.
I heard and you disturbed my belly,   (16)
 by a sound which tingles my lips;
Rottenness is entering my bones,
 and I am disturbed for my sake.
I will rest in the day of trouble
 arising for the people who attack us.
For if the fig tree does not blossom   (17)
 and there be no produce on the vines,
The produce of the olive fail,
 and terraces not give food,
The flock be cut off from the pen
 and there be no herd in the stalls;
Yet I will rejoice in Yahweh,   (18)
 I will exult in the God of my salvation.

Yahweh, my Lord, is my strength,
and he makes my feet like the deer,
and upon the heights he lets me tread.

Habakkuk's Religious Experience: Theophany and History

Is it possible for us to discover what experiences of Habakkuk lie behind the poetic description of the coming of God in this Psalm? What was actually happening when an Israelite was led to speak of a theophany? These are the next questions we need to ask before we are ready to see how the three chapters of this book belong together and before we can consider the magnificent lines with which it concludes. The theophanies of the Old Testament certainly describe appearances of God which have not been witnessed by many, if any, of us. What is really meant by this talk of smoke, fire, and thunder? Is it merely poetic imagery used to express inner feelings? Does it describe something that really did happen, once, at Mount Sinai in a volcanic eruption or something of the sort; something which is then recalled again and again in other circumstances? Did it really happen before the eyes of Israelite worshippers in Jerusalem, with the temple filling with smoke and rocking on its foundations from time to time? I'd like to know.

It is very hard for us to be sure what this theophany-language really refers to, but there is a suggestion made by J. H. Eaton which seems to me to be a very likely possibility, and one I would like to explore. There were visionary types in ancient Israel, people who saw things that others didn't. The prophets, probably all of them, were visionaries. Isaiah and Ezekiel have recorded visions of the appearance of God to them which are parallel in important ways to the theophanies. Isaiah's vision (chap. 6) took place in the temple. He experienced earthquake ("the foundations of the thresholds shook"), smoke ("the house was filled with smoke"), fire ("having in his hand a burning coal"), and a booming voice (vs. 4). That this was an inner, visionary experience and not something that could have been filmed by a movie camera located behind Isaiah is not explicitly stated in this chapter, but it is strongly suggested and the suggestion is supported by Ezekiel's use of "visions of God" to describe similar experiences (Ezek. 8:3). The latter prophet's encounters with God, described in chapters 1 and 10 of his book, involved wind, cloud, fire (1:4, 13f., 27), and a voice like thunder (1:24). Furthermore, the reaction of both prophets to such an experience was fear, dismay, and physical weakness, identical to Habakkuk's reaction in vs. 16.

It seems to me likely, then, that certain visionary personalities in Israel experienced from time to time immensely powerful, physically overwhelming encounters with God in which the most terrifying natural phenomena became the modes of expression of that experience. At any rate, such phenomena provided the most adequate set of words the visionary could find to talk about what had happened. Often the experience probably occurred in worship and it certainly must have happened to some of the cultic personnel who served in the temple, prophets and singers, for it is in the literature produced by such people that theophany is most prominent. Perhaps, then, these visionaries not only shared their experiences with their fellow worshippers but also put them in the form of hymns, laments, and thanksgivings which could then become a part of the worship experience of the whole congregation. Since the physical reaction to so direct an experience of the presence of God seems to have been so profound (cf. also Dan. 8:17, 27; 10:9–11, 15–19), producing fear, weakness, and even fainting, it appears that the most powerful language at one's disposal had to be used in order to convey the effect. This may provide a partial explanation for some of the statements which tend to disturb us, in which God is described as a terrible warrior with pestilence and plague in his train and the bloody bodies of his enemies lying round about. But there is another tradition in Israel which also suggested the use of language like that, and this brings us back again to history.

Habakkuk had a vision—what does that mean beyond being terrifying to the one who experiences it and mystifying to those who have never known such things? The vision has meaning, to the prophet and to his people, because he can identify the God he has encountered as the God of the Exodus. He recognizes this God as more than fire and smoke because this God has revealed his true nature by things he has done for his people in history. This God is the one who brought Israel out of bondage in the land of Egypt (the wonder at the sea recalled in vss. 8, 13–15), led them through the wilderness safely (Teman and Paran) and brought them safely to rest in the Promised Land (Cushan and Midian). Habakkuk speaks of a God who is *known*, not through visions primarily (and thus only to visionaries, primarily) but through events in history which the whole people have experienced and remember. This is the essence of the Israelite belief in God; that he is known through what he has done. So theology-writing, for Israel, is primarily history-writing.

So it is with Christians. We have produced our philosophical theologies a plenty, it is true, and we have our mystics. But when we come to the essence of what God really means to us, we talk about the life and death of a man who lived on this earth in a datable period of our history, of Jesus, his birth, career, how he died, and of his resurrection from the dead. For how else do we know about God, really? He provides no theophanies for us in our churches. When we gather we do not see him or hear him speak aloud. But we know God by what he *has done*, and on that basis we believe in what he will do, in the future. When questions arise about God, about whether he even exists or about whether he cares anything for his people if he does exist, the way we answer such questions is to remember real events from the past, and those things that really happened —which we believe God was responsible for—give us something to depend on that is more than speculation. Whatever anyone may say about God, his existence or his nature, there *was* an

Exodus and there *was* a Jesus of Nazareth, and nothing can change that. So on history we build our theology, and this we Christians have learned from Israel.

When the Fig Tree Does Not Blossom . . .

We are nearly finished. God has not answered Habakkuk's questions in rational terms. But he has *come*. As the coming of God in the book of Job answered none of Job's questions but provided instead a whole new perspective on it all, so the coming of God to Habakkuk confirms his belief that the God of the Exodus is the living God and gives him strength to remain faithful, in spite of anything that may come.

> For if the fig tree does not blossom
>> and there be no produce on the vines,
>
> The produce of the olive fail,
>> and terraces not give food,
>
> The flock be cut off from the pen
>> and there be no herd in the stalls;
>
> Yet I will rejoice in Yahweh,
>> I will exult in the God of my salvation.

What Habakkuk says now is that things may very well become even worse than they were when he was led to complain as he did in chapter 1. He now talks about complete crop failure and the loss of all the livestock. Perhaps he thinks of drought or of the effects of a locust plague; more likely for Habakkuk's time, I should think, he is talking about the way invading armies live off the land, taking everything for themselves as they go and leaving the inhabitants behind to starve. At any rate, there is no doubt that he is talking about starvation. He has covered the agricultural economy of Palestine rather thoroughly in vs. 17: figs, grapes, olives, small grain, sheep, goats and cattle; there was not much else to eat. And this man who had been complaining so bitterly to God about all that is wrong with this world now says: Even though I starve to death, YET I WILL REJOICE IN THE LORD.

These words haunt me more than any other in the Bible. I have often thought about putting them up on the wall of my study as a motto but have never done it, partly because I am not at all sure that is where they belong—up on a wall as a slogan when they ought to be inside, as one's entire orientation to life—and partly, I guess, because they would mock me when I looked at them. Who can really say that and mean it? Yet some have and do.

I do not think one can really understand Habakkuk 2:4, "The just shall live by his faith," until he begins to comprehend 3:17–18. For, what is faith? The former verse does not say. But these verses make clear what it means to live by faith and to be faithful in our living.

Faithfulness means to go on doing the right thing, no matter what happens. Whether anybody ever rewards you or not—do the right thing, because that is what God wants.

Faith means that you don't do it as a sour duty, gritting your teeth like a stoic. Faith means that you *know* the God who puts these demands upon you, and to know God makes you rejoice, no matter what.

Frankly, I don't know if I could rejoice in the Lord in the face of starvation, and I suppose that is why I don't have these verses on my wall as a motto. But they challenge me constantly with the promise that I have a God so great that *nothing* can ever happen which should decrease my joy in knowing him. I don't know whether I can ever really live up to that promise, but some have.

Donald G. Miller, in a sermon on Habakkuk 3:17–18, recalled this incident: John Bunyan was in Bedford jail, imprisoned for his faith and facing a possible death sentence. He was afraid to die. But what bothered him more was that if he showed this fear to the public it might bring discredit on the gospel. And he wrote:

I thought with myself, if I should make a scrabbling shift to clamber up the Ladder, yet I should either with quaking, or other symptoms of fainting, give occasion to the Enemy to reproach the Way of God and his People for their timorousness. This therefore lay with great trouble upon me, for methought I was ashamed to die with a pale Face and tottering Knees, for such a cause as this.

He admitted also his uncertainty about his own salvation, even though he might be dying for his faith, but finally he concluded:

I am for going on, and venturing my eternal state with Christ, whether I have comfort here or no. If God doth not come in, thought I, I will leap off the Ladder even blindfold into Eternity, sink or swim, come Heaven, come Hell. Lord Jesus, if thou wilt catch me, do; if not, I will venture for thy Name.

No better commentary on Habakkuk 2:4 could be asked, although these quotes do not take us to Habakkuk's final state of rejoicing. We have learned that faithfulness means doing what is right no matter what—even Hell. And that faith is the certainty that Jesus is there, no matter what. Habakkuk learned further that the result of this is a kind of incredulous joy that we are *more* than conquerors.

Who shall separate us from the love of Christ?
Shall tribulation, or distress, or persecution,
or famine, or nakedness, or peril, or sword? . . .
No, in all these things we are more than conquerors through
him who loved us.   (ROM. 8:35, 37)

Does "more than conquerors" mean "conquerors and then some" or "not conquerors, but something better"? The English expression might mean either, but a look at the Greek text of Romans makes it clear that Paul was saying the former, since the word he used really means "overwhelming victory is ours" (as the New English Bible rendered it). Yet what we have learned from Habakkuk suggests that the other nuance of the English expression is worth further consideration, for although it is not exactly what

Paul was saying it is a part of the Biblical message. Often we do
not conquer tribulation and distress, physically; they continue to
afflict us whether we are believers or not and we must, like Habakkuk, admit that things may get even worse. Paul and Habakkuk
agree that when we are not yet conquerors at all we have something better—"afflicted in every way, but not crushed; perplexed,
but not driven to despair; persecuted, but not forsaken; struck
down, but not destroyed; always carrying in the body the death
of Jesus, so that the life of Jesus may also be manifested in our
bodies." (2 Cor. 4:8–10)

That is not to ignore the fact that the Bible often promises
us *physical* deliverance—from captivity, from illness, etc.—and
we must take those promises seriously. It is only because Habakkuk believed them that he uttered his cries of anguish over the
suffering of the righteous. It is only for those who really believe
that God intends to give us physical deliverance from evil that the
question, "What if deliverance does not come?" becomes deadly
serious. In wrestling with that question they may lose their faith,
or may win through to something better. The significance of
Habakkuk's ultimate position, we recognize, becomes far more
clear eventually in the Cross of Christ, which demonstrates that
when deliverance does not come the promise of God to be *with
us* is not therefore left unfulfilled. He is with us *in the midst of
trouble,* precisely when we need him most. Though he may not
remove the trouble from us, for reasons we do not understand, still
he enables us to bear it without being beaten down by it, and to
live with it—because he is with us in its very midst.

> When through the deep waters I call thee to go,
> The rivers of sorrow shall not overflow;
> For I will be near thee, thy troubles to bless,
> And sanctify to thee thy deepest distress.
>
>   (From the hymn, "How Firm a Foundation")

I want to return eventually to the value which this promise that
Christ is *with us* in suffering has for us, but for now it is more

important to consider further how the New Testament supports
and enlarges on Habakkuk's curious combination of joy and suffering. For such a mixture may seem less a paradox than utter
nonsense, apart from the Cross.

That joy of which the prophet speaks appears in the New
Testament over and over again in what might seem to be the most
incongruous places:

> Happy are those who mourn: God will comfort them!
>
> Happy are those who suffer persecution because they do what God
> requires: the Kingdom of Heaven belongs to them!
>
> Happy are you when men insult you and mistreat you and tell all
> kinds of evil lies against you because you are my followers.
> Rejoice and be glad, because a great reward is kept for you in
> heaven. This is how men mistreated the prophets who lived
> before you.
>
> (MATT. 5:4, 10, 11; Today's English Version of the New
> Testament)
>
> Then they [the apostles] left the presence of the council, rejoicing
> that they were counted worthy to suffer dishonor for the name.
>
> (ACTS 5:41)
>
> . . . looking to Jesus the pioneer and perfecter of our faith, who
> for the joy that was set before him endured the cross. . . .
>
> (HEB. 12:2)

These, plus many other texts which could be cited, reveal to us
that Habakkuk's joyous exclamation may not be dismissed as an
individual peculiarity inaccessible to the rest of us, for that affirmation has brought us to the heart of the gospel, which is, after
all, "good news of great joy (Luke 2:10)." The gospel itself promises that with God there is a joy that transcends all other human
experience, and that joy may be ours. Not that it makes suffering
any less painful; Jesus himself descended to the depths of human
agony on the cross, including separation from God the Father as
a condemned sinner ("My God, my God, why hast thou forsaken
me?" [Matt. 27:46]; "Christ redeemed us from the curse of the
law, having become a curse for us—for it is written, 'Cursed be

every one who hangs on a tree' " [Gal. 3:13]; cf. Phil. 2:7–8, Heb. 2:9–18). But in the midst of that he had access to a power which enabled him to triumph over pain; as the text from Hebrews quoted earlier says, ". . . who for the joy that was set before him endured the cross, *despising the shame . . .*" It is a joy which cannot be smothered by suffering, which soars above it and draws the human spirit to the God who is pure joy.

James D. Ross' book, *Margaret,* tells the story of his 15-year-old sister-in-law who developed a rare form of cancer which killed her four months after it was discovered. He describes how her family at first tried to protect her from the knowledge of what she had, but when they finally saw she had to be told, her response and subsequent behavior for the remaining months of her life brought about profound changes in the lives of all who knew her. Ross himself was led from agnosticism to a deep Christian faith as he saw that her faith enabled her, within five minutes of learning that she was dying of cancer, to accept what was coming "with peace and joy!" Any incredulity one might feel at reading Habakkuk's words fades in the light of such an account (and it could be repeated for we know not how many others) of a girl struggling with the fatigue and pain which was taking her life and yet holding throughout a tranquility and *humor* grounded in her unwavering faith in Christ. That, I believe, is a part of what is meant by "more than conquerors" and "yet I will rejoice."

But there is a dimension of suffering which is not yet touched by these answers, and it is the one which weighs most heavily in discussions of God's justice. John Bunyan, and you the reader, and Margaret, and I the writer may have found our ways to cope with suffering and become more than conquerors, but we cannot help asking what God has done for the innocents of this world who suffer and know not why. Even if he punishes the wicked, how does that help their victims who know nothing of guilt or punishment? These questions cannot be left without some effort to find an answer, even though it takes us beyond the scope of Habakkuk.

The glimmerings of an answer are to be found in the Old Testament, and it becomes clearer in the Cross, although it is not likely that we can ever hope fully to understand. In parts of the Old Testament the concept of vicarious suffering is introduced; the Servant of the Lord in Isaiah 53 suffers precisely because he is righteous and in doing so takes the suffering of others, who deserve it, upon himself. In Judaism this concept has been used to explain the suffering of innocent children. It was said that, in a generation where there are few that are righteous, the sufferings of the few may atone for the sins of the many; in a generation where none are righteous, the sufferings of children atone for the sins of their elders. In Christianity the concept has been applied to God himself, that in his Son he suffered on the Cross for the redemption of all humanity. This we know well, but we think of it normally as Christ's sufferings *for* the guilty, bearing their sins. Perhaps also Christ suffers *with* the innocent. When a helpless child is being outraged, God is not up in heaven somewhere on a golden throne, he is with and in that child enduring the pain and humiliation as well! He takes all that suffering into himself, and for those of us who know it there is effected a salvation which cannot be touched by anything that can be inflicted on body or mind.

Yet there is a residue of evil which is not erased by God's participation in our daily pain, for not everyone knows that God is there in the midst of his anguish and his salvation is not always experienced. So what Habakkuk promises in chapter 2 cannot be dispensed with. God cannot be just a helpless sufferer, for then nothing at all makes sense. Certainly he loves the wicked as well as the righteous and desires his redemption. He desires not the death of any one (Ezek. 18:23, 32). And yet the evil which afflicts the innocent, which cannot be explained as deserved punishment for sin, or as testing or disciplinary, or as vicarious suffering for others, must be done away with or Habakkuk's question about the justice of God will ultimately have to be answered in the negative. That punishment of the wicked which is described in human terms with such glee in Habakkuk 2 is not finally to be understood as vengeance, or as a failure to recognize that God desires the redemption of everyone, but is an acknowledgment that God must do something more than suffer with that abused child, or he is not in charge after all.

I would like to return to an incident which I recounted earlier in the book as a small illustration of the power of the suffering God. Several years ago the young woman who would one day be my wife was badly injured in a head-on collision. She was in shock for several days and heavily sedated. She had two broken bones which needed to be set, but it was not possible to operate for a week after the accident. On the fourth day they began lessening the amount of sedative she was to receive so that by the fifth day she was out of shock and was alert again. But that fourth day was one of agony for her. She rolled and cried with pain. Her twin sister sat with her and tried to comfort her but gave up in tears. Her father, who was also very close to her, tried to help but he too came out into the hall in tears, asking me to go in. I said a few words to her about Jesus, who suffered on the Cross, who knows what pain feels like, who was there in that room with us then. And I prayed to the suffering Jesus. During that short prayer she became quiet and by the time I had finished she was asleep.

That small incident convinced me, if I needed convincing, that the suffering Christ is with all who suffer—both his pain and his power are there. James Ross revealed how as a new Christian he learned this lesson in his book, *Margaret,* mentioned earlier. Once the agony of his dying sister-in-law moved him to say to her, "You are being crucified like Christ." Later he repeated the statement to the vicar and was told that it was appropriate except for one word. When he altered it and said to Margaret, "You are being crucified with Christ," he had taken a great step in his understanding and experience of the gospel. He reports, "She knew more than I what was meant."

Some years after the death of his sister-in-law, Ross found

another occasion to apply that understanding of the suffering of Christ to an event precisely of the kind to which I have been alluding in these final paragraphs—the suffering of innocents. Edward England, in *The Mountain That Moved*, has written of the tragedy that occurred in 1966 at Aberfan, Wales, when a gigantic coal-tip, loosened by rain, slid into the valley where the village stood, engulfing homes and the Junior School, killing 116 children and 28 adults. As he reports on the effects of so hideous a disaster on those who lost children and those who participated in the rescue efforts, he concludes, ". . . on that hillside, the Cross of Christ assumed a fresh significance. It broke upon a few that Christ was identified with the agony, with the rescuers in intolerable conditions, with those who wept. The Cross seemed suspended above where the miners dug." Then he quotes an editorial concerning the tragedy written by James Ross, which said in part, "We also know one other thing about this disaster, for this is the knowledge which the Christian faith can bring. These children who were buried by that man-made mountain were not alone. Christ was buried with them."

⚓ We cannot explain why we must endure it all. But we know we do not endure it alone for God comes, as Habakkuk learned, and he suffers it all with us, as the Cross reveals, and he makes us more than conquerors. AND I WILL EXULT IN THE GOD OF MY SALVATION.

> Grant, Almighty God, that as thou hast so often and in such various ways testified formerly how much care and solicitude thou hast for the salvation of those who rely and call on thee,—O grant, that we at this day may experience the same: and though thy face is justly hid from us, may we yet never hesitate to flee to thee, since thou hast made a covenant through thy Son, which is founded in thine infinite mercy. Grant then, that we, being humbled in true penitence, may so surrender ourselves to thy Son, that we may be led to thee, and find thee to be no less a Father to us than to the faithful of old, as thou everywhere testifiest to us in thy word, until

at length being freed from all troubles and dangers, we come to
that blessed rest which thy Son has purchased for us by his own
blood. Amen.

(Calvin's prayer at the conclusion of his lecture on Hab. 3:13)

Bibliography

Bradley, I. T. "God's Redeeming Love. Sermon on Hosea 14:4–7," *Perspective* 13 (1972), 118–126.

Bunyan, John. *Grace Abounding to the Chief of Sinners.* London: Hodder & Stoughton, 1888.

Calkins, Raymond. *The Modern Message of the Minor Prophets.* New York: Harper, 1947.

Calvin, John. *Commentaries on the Twelve Minor Prophets.* Volume IV. Grand Rapids: Eerdmans.

Eaton, J. H. "The Origin and Meaning of Habakkuk iii," *Zeitschrift für die Alttestamentliche Wissenschaft* 76 (1964), 144–171.

Elliger, Karl. *Das Buch der zwölf kleinen Propheten.* ("Das Alte Testament Deutsch," Vol. 23, Part 2.) Göttingen: Vandenhoeck & Ruprecht, 1950.

England, Edward. *The Mountain That Moved.* Grand Rapids: Eerdmans, 1967.

Gowan, Donald E. "Habakkuk and Wisdom," *Perspective* 9 (1968), 157–166.

Heschel, Abraham: *Man Is Not Alone: A Philosophy of Religion.* New York: Farrar, Straus & Young, 1951.

Lloyd-Jones, D. M. *From Fear to Faith: Studies in the Book of Habakkuk —and the Problem of History.* London: Inter-Varsity Fellowship, 1953.

Miller, Donald G. "On Rejoicing in God," *Interpretation* 2 (1948), 172–179.

Ross, James D. *Margaret.* London: Hodder & Stoughton, 1957.

Smith, George Adam. *The Book of Isaiah.* Volume I. Garden City: Doubleday, Doran &-Co., 1927.

Smith, George Adam. *The Book of the Twelve Prophets.* Vol. II. Garden City: Doubleday, Doran & Co., 1929.

Vischer, Wilhelm. *Der Prophet Habakuk.* ("Biblische Studien," Vol. 19.) Neukirchen-Vluyn: Neukirchener Verlag. 1958.

Wade, G. W. *The Book of the Prophet Habakkuk.* "Westminster Commentaries." London: Methuen Co., 1929. (Source of the A. L. Barbauld hymn on Hab. 3 quoted at the beginning of Chapter IV.)